Ninja Foodi Smart

DUAL HEAT AIR FRY OVEN

COOKBOOK
FOR BEGINNERS

Simple, Affordable and Delicious Rapid Bake, Toast, Sear Crisp and More Recipes for Anyone to Cook with Smart Air Fry Oven

Jessica Taylor

Table of Contents

INTRODUCTION

Hi there! I'm Jessica Taylor, a mom who knows all too well the struggles of getting kids to eat healthy. But I'm here to share my heartwarming story of how the Ninja Foodi Dual Heat Air Fryer Oven transformed our family's meals and, in the process, brought us closer together.

Like many parents, I faced the challenge of having two children who were madly in love with junk food. Fast food joints and sugary snacks seemed to be their best friends. I watched helplessly as their health and weight suffered, and it broke my heart. I knew I had to make a change, not just for their physical well-being but also to promote a stronger bond within our family.

That's when I discovered the Ninja Foodi Dual Heat Air Fryer Oven. It was a game-changer! This remarkable kitchen appliance offered us a lifeline, a way to enjoy delicious, homemade meals that rivaled their favorite fast-food indulgences. The transformation was incredible. My kids began to fall in love with the delightful meals we prepared together at home, and their weight started to return to normal. But more importantly, we all found joy in cooking, sharing stories, and connecting over the dinner table.

The Ninja Foodi Dual Heat Air Fryer Oven is a powerhouse with its 13 functions, including air roasting, air frying, griddling, dehydrating, baking, and more. It's become the heart of our kitchen, and I'm thrilled to share the delicious recipes that have brought so much happiness to our family.

In this recipe book, you'll find a treasure trove of culinary delights. From rich breakfasts that will make your mornings brighter to crispy snacks that satisfy cravings, we've got you covered. Explore a variety of dehydrated meals for those on-the-go moments, and discover beloved tender fish recipes that will have everyone asking for seconds. Each recipe comes with detailed, step-by-step instructions to make cooking a breeze.

But this book is about more than just recipes; it's about building stronger, more harmonious families. It's about transforming mealtime from a chore into a cherished bonding experience. I wrote this book because I want to help families like mine break free from the grip of junk food and discover the joy of cooking and eating together at home.

So, I invite you to join us on this delicious journey. Let's create a world where families no lon-ger struggle with the allure of unhealthy outside options. Together, we can strengthen family relationships, one meal at a time. Embrace the Ninja Foodi Dual Heat Air Fryer Oven, savor the flavors of home-cooked meals, and rediscover the joy of family time around the table.

Let's cook, eat, and love our way to healthier, happier families. Grab your copy of this recipe book today and let the culinary adventures begin!

CHAPTER 1
BREAKFAST

Creamy Parsley Soufflé

SERVES 2

| PREP TIME: 5 minutes
| COOK TIME: 10 minutes

cooking spray
2 eggs
2 tbsps. light cream
1 tbsp. fresh parsley, chopped
1 fresh red chili pepper, chopped
Salt, to taste

1. Install rack in bottom position, then close door. Select BAKE, set temperature to 390°F, and set time to 10 minutes. Press the setting dial to begin preheating.
2. While unit is preheating, grease 2 soufflé dishes with cooking spray.
3. Mix together all the ingredients in a medium bowl until well combined.
4. Transfer the mixture into prepared soufflé dishes.
5. When unit has preheated, open door and place soufflé dishes onto the center of the rack. Close door to begin cooking.
6. After 10 minutes, check soufflés for doneness by sticking a toothpick in the center of the soufflés. If it comes out clean, remove from oven.
7. When cooking is complete, carefully remove soufflé dishes from the oven. Let cool for 5 minutes before serving.

Ham and Corn Muffins

MAKES 8 MUFFINS

| PREP TIME: 10 minutes
| COOK TIME: 7 minutes

2 tbsps. canola oil
¾ cup yellow cornmeal
¼ cup flour
½ cup milk
½ cup shredded sharp Cheddar cheese
½ cup diced ham
1½ tsps. baking powder
¼ tsp. salt
1 egg, beaten

1. In a medium bowl, stir together the cornmeal, flour, baking powder, and salt.
2. Add the egg, oil, and milk to dry ingredients and combine well.
3. Stir in the shredded cheese and diced ham.
4. Divide batter among 8 parchment-paper-lined muffin cups. Place the muffin cups on a baking pan.
5. Install rack in bottom position, then close door. Select BAKE, set temperature to 390°F, and set time to 7 minutes. Press the setting dial to begin preheating.
6. When unit has preheated, open door and place the baking pan onto the center of the rack. Close door to begin cooking.
7. After 6 minutes, check muffins for doneness by sticking a toothpick in the center of the muffins. If it comes out clean, remove from oven.
8. When cooking is complete, carefully remove pan from the oven. Serve warm.

Crispy Potato Rosti

SERVES 2

| PREP TIME: 10 minutes
| COOK TIME: 15 minutes

1 tbsp. canola oil
½ pound russet potatoes, peeled and grated roughly
3.5 ounces smoked salmon, cut into slices
2 tbsps. shallots, minced
1 tbsp. chives, chopped finely
⅛ cup cheddar cheese
2 tbsps. sour cream
Salt and black pepper, to taste

1. Grease a pizza pan with the canola oil.
2. Install rack in bottom position, then close door. Select BAKE, set temperature to 365°F, and set time to 15 minutes. Press the setting dial to begin preheating.
3. While unit is preheating, mix together potatoes, shallots, chives, cheese, salt and black pepper in a large bowl until well combined.
4. Transfer the potato mixture into the prepared pizza pan.
5. When unit has preheated, open door and place pan onto the center of the rack. Close door to begin cooking.
6. When cooking is complete, carefully remove pan from the oven. Cut the potato rosti into wedges and top with smoked salmon slices and sour cream to serve.

Vegetable Pizza

SERVES 6

| PREP TIME: 30 minutes
| COOK TIME: 15 minutes

1 prebaked, 12-inch thin whole wheat pizza crust
8 small fresh mushrooms, halved
1 small zucchini, cut into ¼-inch slices
1 small red onion, sliced
1 small red pepper, sliced
1 small yellow pepper, sliced
1 tbsp. white wine vinegar
4 tsps. canola oil, divided
½ tsp. dried basil
2 cups shredded part-skim mozzarella cheese
8 ounces (227 g) pizza sauce
2 small tomatoes, chopped
1 tbsp. water
¼ tsp. sea salt
¼ tsp. pepper

1. In a large bowl, add the zucchini, mushrooms, peppers, onions, vinegar, water, 3 tsps. of oil, and seasonings and mix them together.
2. In a skillet, cook the vegetables over medium heat for 8 minutes until tender, stirring often.
3. Install SearPlate in the bottom level of the unit, then close door. Select FRESH PIZZA, set temperature to 500°F, and set time to 7 minutes. Press the setting dial to begin preheating.
4. While unit is preheating, transfer the pizza crust to a sheet of parchment paper.
5. Brush the crust with the remaining oil and spread with pizza sauce. Sprinkle roasted vegetables, tomatoes, and cheese evenly on top.
6. When unit has preheated, transfer the pizza on the parchment paper to the hot SearPlate. Close door to begin cooking.
7. After 4 minutes of cooking, open door and carefully pull the parchment paper out from under the pizza, allowing the pizza to go directly onto the SearPlate. Close door to finish cooking.
8. When cooking is complete, carefully remove pizza from the hot SearPlate. Let pizza cool for 5 minutes. Enjoy!

Mayonnaise Cheese Sandwiches

SERVES 2

| PREP TIME: 10 minutes
| COOK TIME: 5 minutes

cooking spray
4 white bread slices
½ cup sharp cheddar cheese, grated
½ cup melted butter, softened
1 tbsp. mayonnaise

1. Install SearPlate in the bottom level of the unit, then close door. Select GRIDDLE, set temperature to 355°F, and set time to 5 minutes. Press the setting dial to begin preheating.
2. Spread the mayonnaise and melted butter over one side of each bread slice.
3. Sprinkle the cheese over the buttered side of the 2 slices. Cover with the remaining slices of bread.
4. When unit has preheated, open door, carefully transfer the sandwiches to the hot SearPlate. Spray with cooking spray.
5. Reinstall the SearPlate in the bottom level of the unit and close the door to begin cooking, until the cheese is melted.
6. When cooking is complete, remove the sandwiches from the SearPlate, and serve warm.

Sausage Frittata

SERVES 2

| PREP TIME: 15 minutes
| COOK TIME: 11 minutes

1 tbsp. canola oil
3 jumbo eggs
½ of chorizo sausage, sliced
½ cup frozen corn
1 large potato, boiled, peeled and cubed
2 tbsps. feta cheese, crumbled
Salt and black pepper, to taste

1. Heat the canola oil in a pan over medium heat and add the sausage, corn and potato.
2. Cook for about 6 minutes, stirring well. Transfer the mixture to a greased baking pan.
3. Whisk together eggs with salt and black pepper in a medium bowl. Pour in the whisked eggs over the mixture. Top with the feta cheese.
4. Install rack in bottom position, then close door. Select BAKE, set temperature to 350°F, and set time to 5 minutes. Press the setting dial to begin preheating.
5. When unit has preheated, open door and place pan onto the center of the rack. Close door to begin cooking, until the egg is set.
6. When cooking is complete, carefully remove pan from the oven. Serve hot.

Easy Sausage Pizza

SERVES 4

| PREP TIME: 10 minutes
| COOK TIME: 5 minutes

2 tbsps. ketchup
½ pound (227 g) Mozzarella cheese
1 pita bread
⅓ cup sausage
1 tsp. garlic powder
1 tbsp. canola oil

1. Install SearPlate in the bottom level of the unit, then close door. Select FRESH PIZZA, set temperature to 500°F, and set time to 5 minutes. Press the setting dial to begin preheating.
2. While unit is preheating, spread the ketchup over the pita bread.
3. Top with the sausage and cheese. Sprinkle with the garlic powder and brush with canola oil.
4. When unit has preheated, transfer the pizza to the hot SearPlate. Close door to begin cooking.
5. When cooking is complete, carefully remove pizza from the hot SearPlate. Let pizza cool for 5 minutes, then serve warm.

Bacon Wrapped Sausages

SERVES 4

| PREP TIME: 5 minutes
| COOK TIME: 15 minutes

nonstick spray
9 slices bacon
3 brazilian sausages, cut into 3 equal pieces
1 tbsp. Italian herbs
Salt and ground black pepper, to taste

1. Remove Air Fry Basket from oven. Select AIR FRY, set temperature to 400°F, and set time to 25 minutes. Press the setting dial to begin preheating.
2. While unit is preheating, wrap each slice of bacon around each piece of sausage. Sprinkle with Italian herbs, salt and pepper to taste. Place the sausages in the basket, making sure they are not crowding each other. Spray with nonstick spray.
3. When unit has preheated, open door, install the SearPlate in the bottom level of the unit and the basket in the top level of the unit. Close door to begin cooking, flipping halfway through cooking.
4. When cooking is complete, carefully remove basket from the oven. Serve warm.

Spinach and Egg Cups

SERVES 4

| PREP TIME: 15 minutes
| COOK TIME: 23 minutes

Cooking spray
1 tbsp. canola oil
1 pound fresh baby spinach
4 eggs
7 ounces ham, sliced
4 tsps. milk
Salt and black pepper, to taste

1. Spray 4 ramekins with cooking spray.
2. Heat the canola oil in a pan over medium heat and add the spinach.
3. Sauté for about 3 minutes and drain the liquid completely from the spinach.
4. Divide the spinach evenly into the prepared ramekins and add the ham slices.
5. Crack 1 egg over ham in each ramekin and pour the milk over eggs.
6. Season with salt and black pepper to taste.
7. Install rack in bottom position, then close door. Select BAKE, set temperature to 365°F, and set time to 20 minutes. Press the setting dial to begin preheating.
8. When unit has preheated, open door and place ramekins onto the center of the rack. Close door to begin cooking.
9. When cooking is complete, carefully remove ramekins from the oven. Serve warm.

Onion Omelet

SERVES 2

| PREP TIME: 10 minutes
| COOK TIME: 9-11 minutes

Cooking spray
1 tbsp. canola oil
3 eggs
1 large onion, chopped
2 tbsps. grated Cheddar cheese
½ tsp. soy sauce
Salt and ground black pepper, to taste

1. Spritz a baking pan with cooking spray.
2. Heat the oil in a skillet, and cook the chopped onion for 3-5 minutes, until tender. Transfer to the baking pan.
3. Install rack in bottom position, then close door. Select BAKE, set temperature to 355°F, and set time to 6 minutes. Press the setting dial to begin preheating.
4. While unit is preheating, whisk together the eggs, salt, black pepper and soy sauce in a bowl. Pour the egg mixture on top of the onion to coat well. Top with the cheese.
5. When unit has preheated, open door and place pan onto the center of the rack. Close door to begin cooking, until the egg is set.
6. When cooking is complete, carefully remove pan from the oven. Allow to cool before serving.

CHAPTER 2
POULTRY

Lemon Chicken and Spinach Salad

SERVES 4

| PREP TIME: 10 minutes
| COOK TIME: 20 minutes

3 (5-ounce / 142-g) low-sodium boneless, skinless chicken breasts, cut into 1-inch cubes
5 tsps. canola oil
½ tsp. dried thyme
1 medium red onion, sliced
1 red bell pepper, sliced
1 small zucchini, cut into strips
3 tbsps. freshly squeezed lemon juice
6 cups fresh baby spinach

1. Install SearPlate in the bottom level of the unit, then close door. Select SEAR CRISP, set temperature to 400°F, and set time to 20 minutes. Press the setting dial to begin preheating.
2. While unit is preheating, mix the chicken with the canola oil and thyme in a large bowl. Toss to coat well.
3. When unit has preheated, open door, carefully remove the SearPlate with oven mitts and place on top of oven. Place the chicken on the left side, red onion, red bell pepper and zucchini on the right.
4. Reinstall the SearPlate in the bottom level of the unit and close the door to begin cooking, stirring once during cooking, or until the chicken reaches an internal temperature of 165°F (74°C).
5. When cooking is complete, remove the chicken and vegetables from the SearPlate and stir in the lemon juice.
6. Put the spinach in a serving bowl and top with the chicken mixture. Toss to combine well and serve immediately.

Spiced Chicken Breasts

SERVES 4

| PREP TIME: 20 minutes
| COOK TIME: 20 minutes

2 tbsps. coconut butter
4 (6-ounces) boneless, skinless chicken breasts
¼ tsp. onion powder
¼ tsp. garlic powder
¼ tsp. smoked paprika
Salt and black pepper, as required

1. Install SearPlate in the bottom level of the unit, then close door. Select SEAR CRISP, set temperature to 400°F, and set time to 20 minutes. Press the setting dial to begin preheating.
2. While unit is preheating, mix the coconut butter and spices in a medium bowl and coat the chicken with this mixture.
3. When unit has preheated, open door, carefully remove the SearPlate with oven mitts and place on top of oven. Place the chicken breasts on the SearPlate.
4. Reinstall the SearPlate in the bottom level of the unit and close the door to begin cooking, flipping once in between.
5. When cooking is complete, remove the chicken from the SearPlate and serve hot.

Almond-Crusted Chicken Nuggets

SERVES 4

| PREP TIME: 10 minutes
| COOK TIME: 12 minutes

nonstick spray
1 pound (454 g) low-sodium boneless, skinless chicken breasts, cut into 1½-inch cubes
½ cup ground almonds
2 slices low-sodium whole-wheat bread, crumbled
1 egg white
1 tbsp. freshly squeezed lemon juice
½ tsp. dried basil
½ tsp. ground paprika

1. In a shallow bowl, beat the egg white, lemon juice, basil, and paprika with a fork until foamy.
2. Add the chicken and stir to coat well.
3. Mix the almonds and bread crumbs on a plate.
4. Toss the chicken cubes in the almond and bread crumb mixture until well coated.
5. Remove Air Fry Basket from oven. Select AIR FRY, set temperature to 400°F, and set time to 12 minutes. Press the setting dial to begin preheating.
6. While unit is preheating, arrange chicken pieces in the basket, making sure they are not crowding each other. Spray with nonstick spray.
7. When unit has preheated, open door, install the SearPlate in the bottom level of the unit and the basket in the top level of the unit. Close door to begin cooking until the chicken reaches an internal temperature of 165°F on a meat thermometer, shaking halfway through cooking.
8. When cooking is complete, carefully remove basket from the oven. Serve immediately.

Merguez Meatballs

SERVES 4

| PREP TIME: 10 minutes
| COOK TIME: 10 minutes

nonstick spray
1 pound (454 g) ground chicken
2 garlic cloves, finely minced
1 tbsp. sweet Hungarian paprika
1 tsp. kosher salt
1 tsp. ground cumin
1 tsp. coconut sugar
½ tsp. ground fennel
½ tsp. ground coriander
½ tsp. cayenne pepper
½ tsp. black pepper
¼ tsp. ground allspice

1. In a large bowl, mix the chicken, sugar, cumin, garlic, paprika, salt, black pepper, fennel, coriander, cayenne, and allspice until all the ingredients are incorporated.
2. Let stand for about 30 minutes at room temperature, or cover and refrigerate for up to 24 hours.
3. Remove Air Fry Basket from oven. Select AIR FRY, set temperature to 400°F, and set time to 10 minutes. Press the setting dial to begin preheating.
4. While unit is preheating, form the chicken mixture into 16 meatballs. Arrange meatballs in the basket, making sure they are not crowding each other. Spray with nonstick spray.
5. When unit has preheated, open door, install the SearPlate in the bottom level of the unit and the basket in the top level of the unit. Close door to begin cooking, turning halfway through cooking. Use a thermometer to ensure the meatballs have reached an internal temperature of 165°F.
6. When cooking is complete, carefully remove basket from the oven. Serve warm.

Gingered Chicken Drumsticks

SERVES 3

| PREP TIME: 10 minutes
| COOK TIME: 25 minutes

¼ cup full-fat coconut milk
3 (6-ounces) chicken drumsticks
2 tsps. fresh ginger, minced
2 tsps. galangal, minced
2 tsps. ground turmeric
Salt, to taste

1. Mix the coconut milk, galangal, ginger, and spices in a medium bowl.
2. Add the chicken drumsticks and coat generously with the marinade.
3. Refrigerate to marinate for at least 8 hours.
4. Install SearPlate in the bottom level of the unit, then close the door. Select AIR ROAST, set temperature to 390°F, and set time to 25 minutes. Press the setting dial to begin preheating.
5. When unit has preheated, open door and use oven mitts to remove SearPlate and place it on top of oven. Transfer the chicken drumsticks to the SearPlate.
6. Reinstall the SearPlate in the bottom level of the unit. Close door to begin cooking, flipping halfway through cooking.
7. When cooking is complete, carefully remove SearPlate from oven with oven mitts.
8. Transfer the chicken drumsticks onto a serving platter.

BBQ Chicken Wings

SERVES 4

| PREP TIME: 10 minutes
| COOK TIME: 30 minutes

nonstick spray
2 pounds chicken wings, cut into drumettes and flats
½ cup BBQ sauce

1. Remove Air Fry Basket from oven. Select AIR FRY, set temperature to 400°F, and set time to 30 minutes. Press the setting dial to begin preheating.
2. While unit is preheating, arrange chicken wings in the basket, making sure they are not crowding each other. Spray with nonstick spray.
3. When unit has preheated, open door, install the SearPlate in the bottom level of the unit and the basket in the top level of the unit. Close door to begin cooking, flipping halfway through cooking.
4. When cooking is complete, carefully remove basket from the oven. Transfer the chicken wings onto a serving platter and drizzle with the BBQ sauce to serve.

Breaded Chicken Breasts

SERVES 2

| PREP TIME: 20 minutes
| COOK TIME: 22 minutes

nonstick spray
2 tbsps. vegetable oil
2 (6-ounces) chicken breasts
1 egg, beaten
¼ cup Parmesan cheese, grated
4 ounces breadcrumbs
1 tbsp. fresh basil
¼ cup pasta sauce

1. Whisk the egg in a bowl and mix breadcrumbs, vegetable oil and basil in another bowl.
2. Dip the chicken breasts into the egg and then coat evenly with the breadcrumb mixture.
3. Remove Air Fry Basket from oven. Select AIR FRY, set temperature to 350°F, and set time to 22 minutes. Press the setting dial to begin preheating.
4. While unit is preheating, arrange chicken breasts in the basket, making sure they are not crowding each other. Spray with nonstick spray.
5. When unit has preheated, open door, install the SearPlate in the bottom level of the unit and the basket in the top level of the unit. Close door to begin cooking.
6. After 15 minutes, open the door and top the chicken breasts with pasta sauce and Parmesan cheese. Close door to finish cooking.
7. When cooking is complete, carefully remove basket from the oven. Serve immediately.

Chicken and Pepper Kabobs

SERVES 4

| PREP TIME: 20 minutes
| COOK TIME: 12 minutes

4 (4-ounces) skinless, boneless chicken thighs, cubed into 1-inch size
2 bell peppers, cut into 1-inch pieces lengthwise
¼ cup light soy sauce
Wooden skewers, presoaked
1 tbsp. mirin
1 tsp. garlic salt
1 tsp. sugar

1. Mix the soy sauce, mirin, garlic salt, and sugar in a large baking dish.
2. Thread the chicken cubes and bell peppers onto presoaked wooden skewers.
3. Coat the skewers generously with marinade and refrigerate for about 3 hours.
4. Install SearPlate in the bottom level of the unit, then close the door. Select AIR ROAST, set temperature to 375°F, and set time to 12 minutes. Press the setting dial to begin preheating.
5. When unit has preheated, open door and use oven mitts to remove SearPlate and place it on top of oven. Transfer the skewers to the SearPlate.
6. Reinstall the SearPlate in the bottom level of the unit. Close door to begin cooking, flipping halfway through cooking.
7. When cooking is complete, carefully remove SearPlate from oven with oven mitts. Serve warm.

Honey Glazed Chicken Drumsticks

SERVES 4

| PREP TIME: 15 minutes
| COOK TIME: 20 minutes

2 tbsps. canola oil
½ tbsp. fresh rosemary, minced
4 (6-ounces) boneless chicken drumsticks
1 tbsp. fresh thyme, minced
¼ cup Dijon mustard
1 tbsp. honey
Salt and black pepper, to taste

1. Mix the mustard, honey, oil, herbs, salt, and black pepper in a medium bowl.
2. Rub the chicken drumsticks with marinade and refrigerate overnight.
3. Install SearPlate in the bottom level of the unit, then close the door. Select AIR ROAST, set temperature to 390°F, and set time to 20 minutes. Press the setting dial to begin preheating.
4. When unit has preheated, open door and use oven mitts to remove SearPlate and place it on top of oven. Transfer the drumsticks to the SearPlate.
5. Reinstall the SearPlate in the bottom level of the unit. Close door to begin cooking, flipping halfway through cooking.
6. When cooking is complete, carefully remove SearPlate from oven with oven mitts. Transfer the chicken drumsticks onto a serving platter and serve hot.

Cajun Chicken Thighs

SERVES 4

| PREP TIME: 15 minutes
| COOK TIME: 25 minutes

nonstick spray
4 (4-ounces) skin-on chicken thighs
1 egg
½ cup all-purpose flour
1½ tbsps. Cajun seasoning
1 tsp. seasoning salt

1. Mix the flour, Cajun seasoning and salt in a small bowl.
2. Whisk the egg in another bowl and coat the chicken thighs with the flour mixture.
3. Dip into the egg and dredge again into the flour mixture.
4. Remove Air Fry Basket from oven. Select AIR FRY, set temperature to 390°F, and set time to 25 minutes. Press the setting dial to begin preheating.
5. While unit is preheating, arrange chicken thighs in the basket, skin side down, making sure they are not crowding each other. Spray with nonstick spray.
6. When unit has preheated, open door, install the SearPlate in the bottom level of the unit and the basket in the top level of the unit. Close door to begin cooking, flipping halfway through cooking.
7. When cooking is complete, carefully remove basket from the oven. Serve hot.

CHAPTER 3
FISH AND SEAFOOD

Breaded Flounder

SERVES 3

| PREP TIME: 15 minutes
| COOK TIME: 12 minutes

nonstick spray
¼ cup vegetable oil
3 (6-ounces) flounder fillets
1 egg
1 cup dry breadcrumbs
1 lemon, sliced

1. Whisk the egg in a shallow bowl and mix breadcrumbs and oil in another bowl.
2. Dip the flounder fillets into the whisked egg and coat with the breadcrumb mixture.
3. Remove Air Fry Basket from oven. Select AIR FRY, set temperature to 360°F, and set time to 12 minutes. Press the setting dial to begin preheating.
4. While unit is preheating, arrange flounder fillets in the basket, making sure they are not crowding each other. Spray with nonstick spray.
5. When unit has preheated, open door, install the SearPlate in the bottom level of the unit and the basket in the top level of the unit. Close door to begin cooking, flipping halfway through cooking.
6. When cooking is complete, carefully remove basket from the oven. Transfer the flounder fillets onto serving plates and garnish with the lemon slices to serve.

Spicy Orange Shrimp

SERVES 4

| PREP TIME: 20 minutes
| COOK TIME: 10 minutes

nonstick spray
1 pound (454 g) medium shrimp, peeled and deveined, with tails off
⅓ cup orange juice
3 tsps. minced garlic
¼ to ½ tsp. cayenne pepper
1 tsp. Old Bay seasoning

1. In a medium bowl, combine the garlic, orange juice, Old Bay seasoning, and cayenne pepper.
2. Pat the shrimp dry with paper towels.
3. Add the shrimp to the marinade and toss to coat well. Cover with plastic wrap and place in the refrigerator for 30 minutes so the shrimp can soak up the marinade.
4. Remove Air Fry Basket from oven. Select AIR FRY, set temperature to 400°F, and set time to 10 minutes. Press the setting dial to begin preheating.
5. While unit is preheating, arrange shrimp in the basket, making sure they are not crowding each other. Spray with nonstick spray.
6. When unit has preheated, open door, install the SearPlate in the bottom level of the unit and the basket in the top level of the unit. Close door to begin cooking until the shrimp are opaque and crisp, flipping halfway through cooking.
7. When cooking is complete, carefully remove basket from the oven. Serve immediately.

Shrimp Kebabs

SERVES 2

| PREP TIME: 15 minutes
| COOK TIME: 10 minutes

cooking spray
¾ pound shrimp, peeled and deveined
2 tbsps. fresh lemon juice
1 tbsp. fresh cilantro, chopped
Wooden skewers, presoaked
1 tsp. garlic, minced
½ tsp. ground cumin
½ tsp. paprika
Salt and ground black pepper, as required

1. Mix the lemon juice, garlic, cumin and paprika in a medium bowl.
2. Stir in the shrimp and mix to coat well. Season with salt and pepper to taste.
3. Thread the shrimp onto presoaked wooden skewers.
4. Install SearPlate in the bottom level of the unit, then close the door. Select AIR ROAST, set temperature to 350°F, and set time to 10 minutes. Press the setting dial to begin preheating.
5. When unit has preheated, open door and use oven mitts to remove SearPlate and place it on top of oven. Transfer the skewers to the SearPlate and spray with cooking spray.
6. Reinstall the SearPlate in the bottom level of the unit. Close door to begin cooking, flipping halfway through cooking.
7. When cooking is complete, carefully remove SearPlate from oven with oven mitts. Transfer the skewers onto serving plates and serve garnished with fresh cilantro.

Prawn Burgers

SERVES 2

| PREP TIME: 20 minutes
| COOK TIME: 6 minutes

nonstick spray
½ cup prawns, peeled, deveined and finely chopped
½ cup breadcrumbs
2-3 tbsps. onion, finely chopped
½ tsp. ginger, minced
½ tsp. ground cumin
½ tsp. garlic, minced
½ tsp. spices powder
¼ tsp. ground turmeric
3 cups fresh baby greens
Salt and ground black pepper, as required

1. Mix the prawns, breadcrumbs, onion, ginger, garlic, and spices in a medium bowl.
2. Make small-sized patties from the mixture.
3. Remove Air Fry Basket from oven. Select AIR FRY, set temperature to 390°F, and set time to 6 minutes. Press the setting dial to begin preheating.
4. While unit is preheating, arrange patties in the basket, making sure they are not crowding each other. Spray with nonstick spray.
5. When unit has preheated, open door, install the SearPlate in the bottom level of the unit and the basket in the top level of the unit. Close door to begin cooking, flipping halfway through cooking.
6. When cooking is complete, carefully remove basket from the oven. Serve immediately warm alongside the baby greens.

Mahi Mahi with Green Beans

SERVES 4

| PREP TIME: 15 minutes
| COOK TIME: 15 minutes

1 tbsp. avocado oil
5 cups green beans
4 (6-ounces) Mahi Mahi fillets
Salt, as required
2 tbsps. fresh dill, chopped
2 garlic cloves, minced
2 tbsps. fresh lemon juice
1 tbsp. canola oil

1. Install SearPlate in the bottom level of the unit, then close door. Select SEAR CRISP, set temperature to 425°F, and set time to 15 minutes. Press the setting dial to begin preheating.
2. While unit is preheating, mix the green beans, avocado oil and salt in a large bowl.
3. Combine the garlic, dill, lemon juice, salt and canola oil in another bowl. Coat the Mahi Mahi in this garlic mixture.
4. When unit has preheated, open door, carefully remove the SearPlate with oven mitts and place on top of oven. Place the Mahi Mahi on the left side and green beans on the right.
5. Reinstall the SearPlate in the bottom level of the unit and close the door to begin cooking, until the fish is easy flaked by forks and the green beans are tender.
6. When cooking is complete, remove the fish and green beans from the SearPlate. Serve warm.

Garlic-Lemon Tilapia

SERVES 4

| PREP TIME: 5 minutes
| COOK TIME: 12 minutes

1 tbsp. lemon juice
1 tbsp. canola oil
4 (6-ounce / 170-g) tilapia fillets
1 tsp. minced garlic
½ tsp. chili powder

1. Install SearPlate in the bottom level of the unit, then close door. Select SEAR CRISP, set temperature to 380°F, and set time to 12 minutes. Press the setting dial to begin preheating.
2. While unit is preheating, mix together the lemon juice, canola oil, garlic, and chili powder in a large, shallow bowl to make a marinade.
3. Place the tilapia fillets in the bowl and coat evenly.
4. When unit has preheated, open door, carefully remove the SearPlate with oven mitts and place on top of oven. Place the tilapia fillets on the SearPlate.
5. Reinstall the SearPlate in the bottom level of the unit and close the door to begin cooking, until the fish is cooked and flakes easily with a fork.
6. When cooking is complete, remove the fish from the SearPlate and serve hot.

Bacon Wrapped Scallops

SERVES 4

| PREP TIME: 15 minutes
| COOK TIME: 12 minutes

cooking spray
20 sea scallops, cleaned and patted very dry
5 center-cut bacon slices, cut each in 4 pieces
1 tsp. lemon pepper seasoning
½ tsp. paprika
Salt and ground black pepper, to taste

1. Wrap each scallop with a piece of bacon and secure each with a toothpick.
2. Season the scallops evenly with lemon pepper seasoning and paprika.
3. Install SearPlate in the bottom level of the unit, then close the door. Select AIR ROAST, set temperature to 400°F, and set time to 6 minutes. Press the setting dial to begin preheating.
4. When unit has preheated, open door and use oven mitts to remove SearPlate and place it on top of oven. Arrange half of the scallops on the SearPlate. Spray with cooking spray and season with salt and black pepper.
5. Reinstall the SearPlate in the bottom level of the unit. Close door to begin cooking, flipping halfway through cooking.
6. Repeat with the remaining scallops.
7. When cooking is complete, carefully remove SearPlate from oven with oven mitts. Serve warm.

Amazing Salmon Fillets

SERVES 2

| PREP TIME: 5 minutes
| COOK TIME: 12 minutes

cooking spray
2 (7-ounce) (¾-inch thick) salmon fillets
1 tbsp. Italian seasoning
1 tbsp. fresh lemon juice

1. Install SearPlate in the bottom level of the unit, then close door. Select SEAR CRISP, set temperature to 325°F, and set time to 12 minutes. Press the setting dial to begin preheating.
2. While unit is preheating, rub the salmon evenly with Italian seasoning.
3. When unit has preheated, open door, carefully remove the SearPlate with oven mitts and place on top of oven. Place the salmon fillets on the SearPlate, skin-side up. Spray with cooking spray.
4. Reinstall the SearPlate in the bottom level of the unit and close the door to begin cooking, flipping halfway in between, until the fish is cooked and flakes easily with a fork.
5. When cooking is complete, remove the salmon from the SearPlate and squeeze lemon juice on it to serve.

Juicy Salmon and Asparagus Parcels

SERVES 2

| PREP TIME: 5 minutes
| COOK TIME: 13 minutes

1 tsp. canola oil
2 salmon fillets
4 asparagus stalks
¼ cup champagne
Salt and black pepper, to taste
¼ cup white sauce

1. Install SearPlate in the bottom level of the unit, then close the door. Select AIR ROAST, set temperature to 355°F, and set time to 13 minutes. Press the setting dial to begin preheating.
2. Mix all the ingredients in a bowl and divide this mixture evenly over 2 foil papers.
3. When unit has preheated, open door and use oven mitts to remove SearPlate and place it on top of oven. Transfer foil papers to the SearPlate.
4. Reinstall the SearPlate in the bottom level of the unit. Close door to begin cooking.
5. Serve hot.

Crispy Cod Sticks

SERVES 2

| PREP TIME: 20 minutes
| COOK TIME: 7 minutes

nonstick spray
3 (4-ounces) skinless cod fillets, cut into rectangular pieces
4 eggs
¾ cup flour
2 garlic cloves, minced
1 green chili, finely chopped
2 tsps. light soy sauce
Salt and ground black pepper, to taste

1. Place the flour in a shallow dish and whisk the eggs, garlic, green chili, soy sauce, salt, and black pepper in a second dish.
2. Coat the cod fillets evenly in flour then dip in the egg mixture.
3. Remove Air Fry Basket from oven. Select AIR FRY, set temperature to 375°F, and set time to 7 minutes. Press the setting dial to begin preheating.
4. While unit is preheating, arrange cod pieces in the basket, making sure they are not crowding each other. Spray with nonstick spray.
5. When unit has preheated, open door, install the SearPlate in the bottom level of the unit and the basket in the top level of the unit. Close door to begin cooking, flipping halfway through cooking.
6. When cooking is complete, carefully remove basket from the oven. Serve warm.

CHAPTER 4
DEHYDRATED FOODS

Sweet and Sour Chicken Jerky

MAKES ½ POUND JERKY

| **PREP TIME:** 20 minutes
| **COOK TIME:** 6 hours 15 minutes

1½ pounds boneless, skinless chicken breasts, trimmed of all visible fat
1 tbsp. soy sauce
¼ cup pineapple juice
¼ cup firmly packed brown sugar
¼ cup distilled white vinegar
4 fresh garlic cloves, peeled and crushed
1 tbsp. powdered dehydrated onions

1. Partially freeze the chicken breasts, then cut into ¼-inch-thick slices or strips with a very sharp knife. Try to cut them as uniformly as possible for even drying. Place the strips in a large ziptop plastic freezer bag.
2. Whisk the remaining ingredients together in a small bowl and carefully pour over the strips in the bag. Squish everything around to coat, then seal the bag and refrigerate for about 12 hours, turning and squishing the bag about halfway through to ensure even coverage with the marinade.
3. Remove Air Fry Basket from oven. Select DEHYDRATE, set temperature to 150°F, and set time to 6 hours.
4. Drain off the marinade and place the strips in the Air Fry Basket in a single layer. Open door and install the basket in the top position level of the unit. Close door and begin cooking, flipping halfway through cooking. When done, the jerky should bend but not snap.
5. Select AIR FRY, set temperature to 275°F, and set time to 15 minutes. Skip the preheating and begin cooking.
6. When cooking is complete, carefully remove basket from the oven. Enjoy!

Dried Strawberry Slices

SERVES 4

| **PREP TIME:** 20 minutes
| **COOK TIME:** 7 hours

spray bottle of lemon juice
1 pounds strawberries, washed and hulled, then thin sliced

1. Remove Air Fry Basket from oven. Select DEHYDRATE, set temperature to 135°F, and set time to 7 hours.
2. Lightly spray the strawberries with lemon juice. Spread in the Air Fry Basket in a single layer. Open door and install the basket in the top position level of the unit. Close door and begin cooking, flipping halfway through cooking.
3. When cooking is complete, carefully remove basket from the oven. Enjoy!

Smoky Salmon Jerky

MAKES ½ POUND JERKY

| PREP TIME: 30 minutes
| COOK TIME: 6 hours 15 minutes

1½ pounds salmon fillets, skin and pin bones removed
½ cup soy sauce
1 tbsp. Worcestershire sauce
1 tbsp. molasses
1 tbsp. lemon juice
2 tsps. black pepper
1 tsp. liquid smoke

1. Partially freeze the fillets, then cut across into ¼- to ½-inch-thick slices or strips using a very sharp knife or meat slicer. Try to cut the salmon as uniformly as possible for even drying. Place the strips in a large ziptop plastic freezer bag.
2. Whisk the rest of ingredients together in a small bowl and carefully pour over the strips in the bag. Squish everything around to coat, then seal the bag and refrigerate for 3 to 6 hours, turning and squishing the bag about halfway through to ensure even coverage with the marinade.
3. Remove Air Fry Basket from oven. Select DEHYDRATE, set temperature to 150°F, and set time to 6 hours.
4. Drain off the marinade and place the strips in the Air Fry Basket in a single layer. Open door and install the basket in the top position level of the unit. Close door and begin cooking, flipping halfway through cooking. When done, the jerky should bend but not snap.
5. Select AIR FRY, set temperature to 275°F, and set time to 15 minutes. Skip the preheating and begin cooking.
6. When cooking is complete, carefully remove basket from the oven. Enjoy!

Spicy Beef Jerky

MAKES ½ POUND JERKY

| PREP TIME: 20 minutes
| COOK TIME: 6 hours 15 minutes

1½ pounds beef eye of round
½ cup pineapple juice
¼ cup soy sauce
¼ cup firmly packed brown sugar
1 tbsp. crushed dehydrated jalapeños
1 tsp. hot sauce

1. Trim the meat of any visible fat, then partially freeze. Cut into ¼-inch-thick slices or strips across the grain using a very sharp knife. Try to cut the meat as uniformly as possible for even drying. Place the strips in a large ziptop plastic freezer bag.
2. While the meat freezes, combine the remaining ingredients in a small saucepan. Place over medium heat and stir until the sugar dissolves. Let cool, then carefully pour over the strips in the bag. Squish everything around to coat, then seal the bag and refrigerate until the meat is no longer red, about 24 hours, turning and squishing the bag about halfway through to ensure even coverage with the marinade.
3. Remove Air Fry Basket from oven. Select DEHYDRATE, set temperature to 150°F, and set time to 6 hours.
4. Drain off the marinade and place the strips in the Air Fry Basket in a single layer. Open door and install the basket in the top position level of the unit. Close door and begin cooking, flipping halfway through cooking. When done, the jerky should bend but not snap.
5. Select AIR FRY, set temperature to 275°F, and set time to 15 minutes. Skip the preheating and begin cooking.
6. When cooking is complete, carefully remove basket from the oven. Enjoy!

Sriracha Turkey Jerky

MAKES ½ POUND JERKY

| PREP TIME: 15 minutes
| COOK TIME: 7 hours 15 minutes

1½ pounds boneless, skinless turkey breast, trimmed of all visible fat
⅔ cup soy sauce
¼ cup sriracha
3 tbsps. honey
2 tsps. red pepper flakes

1. Partially freeze the turkey breast, then cut into ¼-inch-thick slices or strips with a very sharp knife. Try to cut it as uniformly as possible for even drying. Place the strips in a large ziptop plastic freezer bag.
2. Whisk the rest of ingredients together in a small bowl and carefully pour over the strips in the bag. Squish everything around to coat, then seal the bag and refrigerate for 12 hours, turning and squishing the bag about halfway through to ensure even coverage with the marinade.
3. Remove Air Fry Basket from oven. Select DEHYDRATE, set temperature to 150°F, and set time to 7 hours.
4. Drain off the marinade and place the strips in the Air Fry Basket in a single layer. Open door and install the basket in the top position level of the unit. Close door and begin cooking, flipping halfway through cooking. When done, the jerky should bend but not snap.
5. Select AIR FRY, set temperature to 275°F, and set time to 15 minutes. Skip the preheating and begin cooking.
6. When cooking is complete, carefully remove basket from the oven. Enjoy!

Healthy Dried Kiwi

SERVES 4

| PREP TIME: 20 minutes
| COOK TIME: 8 hours

spray bottle of lemon juice
4 medium kiwi fruits, peeled and sliced as thinly as you can

1. Remove Air Fry Basket from oven. Select DEHYDRATE, set temperature to 135°F, and set time to 8 hours.
2. Lightly spray the kiwi slices with lemon juice and spread in the Air Fry Basket in a single layer. Open door and install the basket in the top position level of the unit. Close door and begin cooking, flipping halfway through cooking.
3. When cooking is complete, carefully remove basket from the oven. Serve immediately.

Dehydrated Asparagus

SERVES 6

| PREP TIME: 20 minutes
| COOK TIME: 8 hours

1 pounds asparagus, washed

1. Remove the tough end, then boil or steam asparagus just until you can pierce the thick end with a knife; don't let it get mushy. Drain, then plunge into a large bowl of ice water until cool. Cut thick stalks into 1- to 3-inch pieces; thin stalks can be left whole.
2. Remove Air Fry Basket from oven. Select DEHYDRATE, set temperature to 135°F, and set time to 8 hours.
3. Place the asparagus in the Air Fry Basket in a single layer. Open door and install the basket in the top position level of the unit. Close door and begin cooking, shaking halfway through cooking.
4. When cooking is complete, carefully remove basket from the oven. Serve immediately.

Tasty Green Olives

SERVES 6

| PREP TIME: 10 minutes **| COOK TIME:** 8 hours	**1 pounds green olives, drained and pitted**

1. Remove Air Fry Basket from oven. Select DEHYDRATE, set temperature to 135°F, and set time to 8 hours.
2. Place the green olives in the Air Fry Basket in a single layer. Open door and install the basket in the top position level of the unit. Close door and begin cooking, shaking halfway through cooking.
3. When cooking is complete, carefully remove basket from the oven. Enjoy!

Homemade Dried Tomato Slices

SERVES 6

| PREP TIME: 20 minutes **| COOK TIME:** 6 hours	**1 pounds large tomatoes, washed and cut into ¼-inch slices**

1. Spread the tomato slices on dehydrator rack.
2. Push in the legs on the Crisper Tray, then place the tray in the bottom position in the pot. Put the rack with tomatoes on the tray.
3. Close the lid and flip the SmartSwitch to AIRFRY/STOVETOP. Select DEHYDRATE, set temperature to 135°F, and set time to 6 hours. Press START/STOP to begin cooking. When done, the tomatoes should feel dry like paper, and be flexible but easily torn.
4. Remove the tomatoes from the cooker, serve immediately ou vacuum seal in vacuum bags with an oxygen pack, and then double-bagged in Mylar bag.

Crispy Dragon Fruit

SERVES 6

| PREP TIME: 20 minutes **| COOK TIME:** 8 hours	**3 large Dragon Fruits, washed thoroughly, cut into ¼-inch slices and left the skin on the fruit (can hold the slices together)**

1. Remove Air Fry Basket from oven. Select DEHYDRATE, set temperature to 135°F, and set time to 8 hours.
2. Place the fruit slices in the Air Fry Basket in a single layer. Open door and install the basket in the top position level of the unit. Close door and begin cooking, flipping halfway through cooking.
3. When cooking is complete, carefully remove basket from the oven. Enjoy!

CHAPTER 5
VEGETABLES

Spicy Potatoes

SERVES 6

| PREP TIME: 10 minutes
| COOK TIME: 20 minutes

nonstick spray
1 tbsp. canola oil
1¾ pounds waxy potatoes, peeled and cubed
½ tsp. ground cumin
½ tsp. ground coriander
½ tsp. paprika
Salt and black pepper, to taste

1. Remove Air Fry Basket from oven. Select AIR FRY, set temperature to 390°F, and set time to 20 minutes. Press the setting dial to begin preheating.
2. While unit is preheating, mix the potatoes, canola oil, and spices in a medium bowl and toss to coat well.
3. Arrange the potatoes in the basket, making sure they are not crowding each other. Spray with nonstick spray.
4. When unit has preheated, open door, install the SearPlate in the bottom level of the unit and the basket in the top level of the unit. Close door to begin cooking, shaking halfway through cooking.
5. When cooking is complete, carefully remove basket from the oven. Transfer the potato cubes onto serving plates and serve hot.

Roasted Eggplant Slices

SERVES 1

| PREP TIME: 5 minutes
| COOK TIME: 15 minutes

2 tbsps. canola oil
1 large eggplant, sliced
¼ tsp. salt
½ tsp. garlic powder

1. Install SearPlate in the bottom level of the unit, then close the door. Select AIR ROAST, set temperature to 390°F, and set time to 15 minutes. Press the setting dial to begin preheating.
2. While unit is preheating, brush with the eggplant slices with canola oil on both sides. Season each side with sprinklings of salt and garlic powder.
3. When unit has preheated, open door and use oven mitts to remove SearPlate and place it on top of oven. Transfer eggplant slices to the SearPlate.
4. Reinstall the SearPlate in the bottom level of the unit. Close door to begin cooking, flipping halfway through cooking.
5. When cooking is complete, carefully remove SearPlate from oven with oven mitts. Serve immediately.

Garlic Broccoli

SERVES 3

| PREP TIME: 15 minutes
| COOK TIME: 18 minutes

1 tbsp. coconut butter
1 large head broccoli, cut into bite-sized pieces
3 garlic cloves, sliced
2 tsps. vegetable bouillon granules
1 tbsp. fresh lemon juice
½ tsp. red pepper flakes, crushed
½ tsp. fresh lemon zest, finely grated

1. In a skillet over medium heat, add the coconut butter, bouillon granules and lemon juice and cook for about 1½ minutes.
2. Stir in the garlic and cook for about 30 seconds. Set aside and add the broccoli, lemon zest, and red pepper flakes and combine well.
3. Install SearPlate in the bottom level of the unit, then close the door. Select AIR ROAST, set temperature to 375°F, and set time to 16 minutes. Press the setting dial to begin preheating.
4. When unit has preheated, open door and use oven mitts to remove SearPlate and place it on top of oven. Transfer broccoli to the SearPlate.
5. Reinstall the SearPlate in the bottom level of the unit. Close door to begin cooking, shaking halfway through cooking.
6. When cooking is complete, carefully remove SearPlate from oven with oven mitts. Transfer to a bowl and serve hot.

Bistro Potato Wedges

SERVES 4

| PREP TIME: 10 minutes
| COOK TIME: 15 minutes

nonstick spray
1 pound (454 g) fingerling potatoes, cut into wedges
1 tsp. extra-virgin canola oil
½ tsp. garlic powder
Salt and pepper, to taste
½ cup raw cashews, soaked in water overnight
1 tsp. fresh lemon juice
1 tbsp. nutritional yeast
½ tsp. ground turmeric
½ tsp. paprika
2 tbsps. to ¼ cup water

1. Remove Air Fry Basket from oven. Select AIR FRY, set temperature to 400°F, and set time to 15 minutes. Press the setting dial to begin preheating.
2. While unit is preheating, toss together the potato wedges, canola oil, garlic powder, and salt and pepper in a medium bowl, making sure to coat the potatoes well.
3. Arrange potato wedges in the basket, making sure they are not crowding each other. Spray with nonstick spray.
4. When unit has preheated, open door, install the SearPlate in the bottom level of the unit and the basket in the top level of the unit. Close door to begin cooking.
5. Meanwhile, prepare the cheese sauce. In a food processor, pulse the cashews, turmeric, paprika, nutritional yeast, lemon juice, and water together. Add more water to achieve your desired consistency.
6. When the potatoes have cooked for 12 minutes, open door and top with cheese sauce. Close door to finish cooking.
7. When cooking is complete, carefully remove basket from the oven. Serve hot.

Lemony Green Beans

SERVES 3

| PREP TIME: 15 minutes
| COOK TIME: 12 minutes

1 pound green beans, trimmed and halved
1 tbsp. fresh lemon juice
1 tsp. coconut butter, melted
¼ tsp. garlic powder

1. Install SearPlate in the bottom level of the unit, then close the door. Select AIR ROAST, set temperature to 425°F, and set time to 12 minutes. Press the setting dial to begin preheating.
2. While unit is preheating, mix all the ingredients in a medium bowl and toss to coat well.
3. When unit has preheated, open door and use oven mitts to remove SearPlate and place it on top of oven. Transfer green beans to the SearPlate.
4. Reinstall the SearPlate in the bottom level of the unit. Close door to begin cooking, shaking halfway through cooking.
5. When cooking is complete, carefully remove SearPlate from oven with oven mitts. Serve hot.

Parmesan Asparagus

SERVES 3

| PREP TIME: 15 minutes
| COOK TIME: 10 minutes

nonstick spray
1 pound fresh asparagus, trimmed
1 tbsp. vegetable oil
1 tbsp. Parmesan cheese, grated
1 tsp. garlic powder
Salt and black pepper, to taste

1. Remove Air Fry Basket from oven. Select AIR FRY, set temperature to 400°F, and set time to 10 minutes. Press the setting dial to begin preheating.
2. While unit is preheating, mix the asparagus, cheese, vegetable oil, garlic powder, salt, and black pepper in a medium bowl and toss to coat well.
3. Arrange asparagus in the basket and spray with nonstick spray.
4. When unit has preheated, open door, install the SearPlate in the bottom level of the unit and the basket in the top level of the unit. Close door to begin cooking, shaking halfway through cooking.
5. When cooking is complete, carefully remove basket from the oven. Transfer the asparagus to a serving plate and serve hot.

Sriracha Golden Cauliflower

SERVES 4

| PREP TIME: 5 minutes
| COOK TIME: 15 minutes

4 cups cauliflower florets
1 cup bread crumbs
¼ cup sriracha sauce
¼ cup vegan butter, melted
1 tsp. salt

1. Mix the sriracha and vegan butter in a small bowl and pour this mixture over the cauliflower to cover each floret entirely.
2. In a separate bowl, combine the bread crumbs and salt.
3. Dip the cauliflower florets in the bread crumbs, coating each one well.
4. Install SearPlate in the bottom level of the unit, then close the door. Select AIR ROAST, set temperature to 390°F, and set time to 15 minutes. Press the setting dial to begin preheating.
5. When unit has preheated, open door and use oven mitts to remove SearPlate and place it on top of oven. Transfer cauliflower florets to the SearPlate.
6. Reinstall the SearPlate in the bottom level of the unit. Close door to begin cooking, shaking halfway through cooking.
7. When cooking is complete, carefully remove SearPlate from oven with oven mitts. Serve hot.

Caramelized Brussels Sprouts

SERVES 4

| PREP TIME: 10 minutes
| COOK TIME: 35 minutes

4 tsps. coconut butter, melted
1 pound Brussels sprouts, trimmed and halved
Salt and black pepper, to taste

1. Install SearPlate in the bottom level of the unit, then close the door. Select AIR ROAST, set temperature to 400°F, and set time to 35 minutes. Press the setting dial to begin preheating.
2. While unit is preheating, mix all the ingredients in a medium bowl and toss to coat well.
3. When unit has preheated, open door and use oven mitts to remove SearPlate and place it on top of oven. Transfer Brussels sprouts to the SearPlate.
4. Reinstall the SearPlate in the bottom level of the unit. Close door to begin cooking, shaking halfway through cooking.
5. When cooking is complete, carefully remove SearPlate from oven with oven mitts. Serve warm.

Easy Glazed Carrots

SERVES 4

| PREP TIME: 10 minutes
| COOK TIME: 15 minutes

1 tbsp. canola oil
1 tbsp. honey
3 cups carrots, peeled and cut into large chunks
Salt and black pepper, to taste

1. Install SearPlate in the bottom level of the unit, then close the door. Select AIR ROAST, set temperature to 425°F, and set time to 15 minutes. Press the setting dial to begin preheating.
2. While unit is preheating, mix all the ingredients in a medium bowl and toss to coat well.
3. When unit has preheated, open door and use oven mitts to remove SearPlate and place it on top of oven. Transfer the carrots to the SearPlate.
4. Reinstall the SearPlate in the bottom level of the unit. Close door to begin cooking, shaking halfway through cooking.
5. When cooking is complete, carefully remove SearPlate from oven with oven mitts. Serve hot.

Crispy Green Beans and Mushroom

SERVES 6

| PREP TIME: 15 minutes
| COOK TIME: 14 minutes

3 tbsps. canola oil
24 ounces fresh green beans, trimmed
2 cups fresh button mushrooms, sliced
⅓ cup French fried onions
2 tbsps. fresh lemon juice
1 tsp. garlic powder
1 tsp. ground sage
1 tsp. onion powder
Salt and black pepper, to taste

1. Install SearPlate in the bottom level of the unit, then close the door. Select AIR ROAST, set temperature to 400°F, and set time to 14 minutes. Press the setting dial to begin preheating.
2. While unit is preheating, mix the green beans, mushrooms, oil, lemon juice, sage, and spices in a medium bowl and toss to coat well.
3. When unit has preheated, open door and use oven mitts to remove SearPlate and place it on top of oven. Transfer the green beans and mushrooms to the SearPlate.
4. Reinstall the SearPlate in the bottom level of the unit. Close door to begin cooking, shaking halfway through cooking.
5. When cooking is complete, carefully remove SearPlate from oven with oven mitts. Transfer the green beans and mushrooms to a serving dish and top with fried onions to serve.

CHAPTER 6
PORK

Breaded Pork Chops

SERVES 2

| PREP TIME: 15 minutes
| COOK TIME: 15 minutes

nonstick spray
1 tbsp. vegetable oil
2 (6-ounces) pork chops
1 egg
4 ounces breadcrumbs
¼ cup plain flour
Salt and black pepper, to taste

1. Season the pork chops with salt and black pepper.
2. Place the flour in a shallow bowl and whisk an egg in a second bowl.
3. Mix the breadcrumbs and vegetable oil in a third bowl.
4. Coat the pork chops with flour, dip into egg and dredge into the breadcrumb mixture.
5. Remove Air Fry Basket from oven. Select AIR FRY, set temperature to 400°F, and set time to 15 minutes. Press the setting dial to begin preheating.
6. While unit is preheating, arrange pork chops in the basket, making sure they are not crowding each other. Spray with nonstick spray.
7. When unit has preheated, open door, install the SearPlate in the bottom level of the unit and the basket in the top level of the unit. Close door to begin cooking, flipping halfway through cooking.
8. When cooking is complete, carefully remove basket from the oven. Serve hot.

Air Fried Baby Back Ribs

SERVES 2

| PREP TIME: 5 minutes
| COOK TIME: 30 minutes

nonstick spray
2 baby back ribs
3 cloves minced garlic
2 tsps. red pepper flakes
¾ ground ginger
Salt and ground black pepper, to taste

1. Remove Air Fry Basket from oven. Select AIR FRY, set temperature to 350°F, and set time to 30 minutes. Press the setting dial to begin preheating.
2. While unit is preheating, combine the red pepper flakes, ginger, garlic, salt and pepper in a small bowl, making sure to mix well. Massage the mixture into the baby back ribs.
3. Arrange ribs in the basket and spray with nonstick spray.
4. When unit has preheated, open door, install the SearPlate in the bottom level of the unit and the basket in the top level of the unit. Close door to begin cooking, flipping halfway through cooking.
5. When cooking is complete, carefully remove basket from the oven. Put the ribs on a serving dish and serve hot.

Pork Tenderloin with Bell Peppers

SERVES 2

| PREP TIME: 20 minutes
| COOK TIME: 15 minutes

1 tbsp. canola oil
10½-ounces pork tenderloin, cut into 4 pieces
1 large red bell pepper, seeded and cut into thin strips
1 red onion, thinly sliced
2 tsps. Herbs de Provence
Salt and ground black pepper, as required
½ tbsp. Dijon mustard

1. Install SearPlate in the bottom level of the unit, then close door. Select SEAR CRISP, set temperature to 400°F, and set time to 15 minutes. Press the setting dial to begin preheating.
2. While unit is preheating, mix the bell pepper, onion, Herbs de Provence, salt, black pepper, and ½ tbsp. of oil in a medium bowl.
3. Rub the tenderloins evenly with mustard, salt, and black pepper and drizzle with the remaining oil.
4. When unit has preheated, open door, carefully remove the SearPlate with oven mitts and place on top of oven. Place the pork tenderloins on the left side and bell pepper mixture on the right.
5. Reinstall the SearPlate in the bottom level of the unit and close the door to begin cooking.
6. When cooking is complete, make sure pork is cooked through with a thermometer. The internal temperature should read 145°F or higher. Transfer the pork and vegetables to a plate and serve.

Sun-dried Tomato Crusted Chops

SERVES 4

| PREP TIME: 15 minutes
| COOK TIME: 10 minutes

cooking spray
4 center-cut boneless pork chops (about 1¼ pounds / 567 g)
½ cup oil-packed sun-dried tomatoes
½ cup canola oil
½ cup toasted almonds
¼ cup grated Parmesan cheese
2 tbsps. water
½ tsp. salt
Freshly ground black pepper, to taste

1. Place the sun-dried tomatoes into a food processor and pulse them until they are coarsely chopped.
2. Add the almonds, canola oil, Parmesan cheese, water, salt and pepper. Process into a smooth paste. Spread most of the paste (leave a little in reserve) onto both sides of the pork chops and then pierce the meat several times with a fork.
3. Let the pork chops sit and marinate for at least 1 hour (refrigerate if marinating for longer than 1 hour).
4. Install SearPlate in the bottom level of the unit, then close door. Select SEAR CRISP, set temperature to 390°F, and set time to 10 minutes. Press the setting dial to begin preheating.
5. When unit has preheated, open door, carefully remove the SearPlate with oven mitts and place on top of oven. Place the pork chops on the SearPlate, spooning a little more of the sun-dried tomato paste onto the pork chops if there are any gaps where the paste may have been rubbed off. Spray with cooking spray.
6. Reinstall the SearPlate in the bottom level of the unit and close the door to begin cooking, flipping halfway through cooking.
7. When cooking is complete, make sure pork is cooked through with a thermometer. The internal temperature should read 145°F or higher. Transfer the pork chops to a serving plate and serve.

Teriyaki Pork and Mushroom Rolls

SERVES 6

| PREP TIME: 10 minutes
| COOK TIME: 10 minutes

nonstick spray
6 (4-ounce / 113-g) pork belly slices
6 ounces (170 g) Enoki mushrooms
4 tbsps. brown sugar
4 tbsps. soy sauce
4 tbsps. mirin
2-inch ginger, chopped
1 tsp. almond flour

1. Mix the brown sugar, mirin, soy sauce, almond flour and ginger together in a small until brown sugar dissolves.
2. Wrap a bundle of mushrooms with each pork belly slice. Brush each roll with teriyaki sauce. Chill for half an hour.
3. Remove Air Fry Basket from oven. Select AIR FRY, set temperature to 375°F, and set time to 10 minutes. Press the setting dial to begin preheating.
4. While unit is preheating, arrange pork rolls in the basket, making sure they are not crowding each other. Spray with nonstick spray.
5. When unit has preheated, open door, install the SearPlate in the bottom level of the unit and the basket in the top level of the unit. Close door to begin cooking, flipping halfway through cooking.
6. When cooking is complete, carefully remove basket from the oven. Serve immediately.

Filling Pork Chops

SERVES 2

| PREP TIME: 20 minutes
| COOK TIME: 14 minutes

2 tbsps. canola oil
2 (1-inch thick) pork chops
½ tbsp. fresh parsley, chopped
½ tbsp. fresh cilantro, chopped
½ tbsp. fresh rosemary, chopped
2 garlic cloves, minced
¾ tbsp. Dijon mustard
1 tbsp. ground coriander
1 tsp. coconut sugar
Salt, to taste

1. Mix all the ingredients in a large bowl except the pork chops.
2. Coat the pork chops with marinade generously and cover to refrigerate for about 3 hours.
3. Keep the pork chops at room temperature for about 30 minutes.
4. Install SearPlate in the bottom level of the unit, then close door. Select SEAR CRISP, set temperature to 400°F, and set time to 14 minutes. Press the setting dial to begin preheating.
5. When unit has preheated, open door, carefully remove the SearPlate with oven mitts and place on top of oven. Place the pork chops on the SearPlate.
6. Reinstall the SearPlate in the bottom level of the unit and close the door to begin cooking, flipping once in between.
7. When cooking is complete, make sure pork is cooked through with a thermometer. The internal temperature should read 145°F or higher. Remove the pork chops from the SearPlate and serve hot.

Potato and Prosciutto Salad

SERVES 8

| **PREP TIME:** 10 minutes
| **COOK TIME:** 7 minutes

For the Salad:
4 pounds (1.8 kg) potatoes, boiled and cubed
15 slices prosciutto, diced
2 cups shredded Cheddar cheese
For the Dressing:
15 ounces (425 g) sour cream
2 tbsps. mayonnaise
1 tsp. dried basil
1 tsp. salt
1 tsp. black pepper

1. Install rack in bottom position. Select BROIL, set temperature to LO, and set time to 7 minutes.
2. Put the potatoes, prosciutto, and Cheddar in a baking dish and arrange onto the center of the rack. Close door to begin cooking.
3. Meanwhile, using a whisk, mix the sour cream, mayonnaise, salt, pepper, and basil in a separate bowl.
4. When cooking is complete, carefully remove dish from the oven. Coat the salad with the dressing and serve.

Marinated Pork Tenderloin

SERVES 4-6

| **PREP TIME:** 10 minutes
| **COOK TIME:** 30 minutes

¼ cup canola oil
2 pounds (907 g) pork tenderloin
¼ cup freshly squeezed lemon juice
¼ cup soy sauce
1 garlic clove, minced
1 tbsp. Dijon mustard
1 tsp. salt
½ tsp. freshly ground black pepper

1. In a large mixing bowl, make the marinade: Mix the canola oil, lemon juice, soy sauce, minced garlic, Dijon mustard, salt, and pepper. Reserve ¼ cup of the marinade.
2. Place the tenderloin in a large bowl and pour the remaining marinade over the meat. Cover and marinate in the refrigerator for about 1 hour.
3. Install SearPlate in the bottom level of the unit, then close door. Select SEAR CRISP, set temperature to 400°F, and set time to 30 minutes. Press the setting dial to begin preheating.
4. When unit has preheated, open door, carefully remove the SearPlate with oven mitts and place on top of oven. Place the pork tenderloins on the SearPlate.
5. Reinstall the SearPlate in the bottom level of the unit and close the door to begin cooking. Flip the pork and baste with half of the reserved marinade twice times.
6. When cooking is complete, make sure pork is cooked through with a thermometer. The internal temperature should read 145°F or higher.
7. Remove the pork from the SearPlate and serve immediately.

Sausage Meatballs

SERVES 4

| PREP TIME: 15 minutes
| COOK TIME: 15 minutes

nonstick spray
3½-ounce sausage, casing removed
½ medium onion, minced finely
3 tbsps. Italian breadcrumbs
1 tsp. fresh sage, chopped finely
½ tsp. garlic, minced
Salt and black pepper, to taste

1. Remove Air Fry Basket from oven. Select AIR FRY, set temperature to 355°F, and set time to 15 minutes. Press the setting dial to begin preheating.
2. While unit is preheating, mix all the ingredients in a medium bowl until well combined.
3. Shape the mixture into equal-sized balls and arrange in the basket, making sure they are not crowding each other. Spray with nonstick spray.
4. When unit has preheated, open door, install the SearPlate in the bottom level of the unit and the basket in the top level of the unit. Close door to begin cooking, shaking halfway through cooking.
5. When cooking is complete, carefully remove basket from the oven. Serve warm.

Herbed Pork Burgers

SERVES 8

| PREP TIME: 15 minutes
| COOK TIME: 22 minutes

21-ounce ground pork
2 small onions, chopped
½ cup cheddar cheese, grated
8 burger buns
2 tsps. fresh basil, chopped
2 tsps. garlic puree
2 tsps. mustard
2 tsps. tomato puree
2 tsps. dried mixed herbs, crushed
Salt and freshly ground black pepper, to taste

1. Mix all the ingredients in a medium bowl except cheese and buns.
2. Shape the pork mixture into 8 equal-sized patties.
3. Remove Air Fry Basket from oven. Select AIR FRY, set temperature to 390°F, and set time to 22 minutes. Press the setting dial to begin preheating.
4. While unit is preheating, arrange patties in the basket, making sure they are not crowding each other. Spray with nonstick spray.
5. When unit has preheated, open door, install the SearPlate in the bottom level of the unit and the basket in the top level of the unit. Close door to begin cooking, flipping halfway through cooking.
6. When cooking is complete, carefully remove basket from the oven. Arrange the patties in buns with cheese to serve.

CHAPTER 7
LAMB

Nut Crusted Rack of Lamb

SERVES 6

| PREP TIME: 15 minutes
| COOK TIME: 15 minutes

nonstick spray
1 tbsp. canola oil
1¾ pounds rack of lamb
1 egg
3-ounce almonds, chopped finely
1 tbsp. breadcrumbs
1 tbsp. fresh rosemary, chopped
1 garlic clove, minced
Salt and black pepper, to taste

1. Mix the canola oil, garlic, salt and black pepper in a small bowl.
2. Whisk the egg in a shallow dish and mix breadcrumbs, almonds and rosemary in another shallow dish.
3. Coat the rack of lamb with garlic mixture evenly, dip into the egg and dredge into the breadcrumb mixture.
4. Remove Air Fry Basket from oven. Select AIR FRY, set temperature to 390°F, and set time to 15 minutes. Press the setting dial to begin preheating.
5. While unit is preheating, arrange rack of lamb in the basket, making sure they are not crowding each other. Spray with nonstick spray.
6. When unit has preheated, open door, install the SearPlate in the bottom level of the unit and the basket in the top level of the unit. Close door to begin cooking, flipping halfway through cooking.
7. When cooking is complete, carefully remove basket from the oven and serve warm.

Fantastic Leg of Lamb

SERVES 4

| PREP TIME: 10 minutes
| COOK TIME: 1 hour

2 tbsps. canola oil
2 pounds leg of lamb
2 fresh rosemary sprigs
2 fresh thyme sprigs
Salt and black pepper, to taste

1. Install SearPlate in the bottom level of the unit, then close the door. Select AIR ROAST, set temperature to 390°F, and set time to 60 minutes. Press the setting dial to begin preheating.
2. While unit is preheating, sprinkle the leg of lamb with oil, salt and black pepper and wrap with herb sprigs.
3. When unit has preheated, open door and use oven mitts to remove SearPlate and place it on top of oven. Transfer leg of lamb to the SearPlate.
4. Reinstall the SearPlate in the bottom level of the unit. Close door to begin cooking, flipping halfway through cooking.
5. When cooking is complete, make sure lamb is cooked through with a thermometer. The internal temperature should read 145°F.
6. Remove SearPlate from oven with oven mitts. Transfer the lamb leg to a plate and serve warm.

Za'atar Lamb Loin Chops

SERVES 4

| PREP TIME: 10 minutes
| COOK TIME: 15 minutes

1 tsp. canola oil
8 (3½-ounces) bone-in lamb loin chops, trimmed
3 garlic cloves, crushed
1 tbsp. fresh lemon juice
1 tbsp. Za'atar
Salt and black pepper, to taste

1. Install SearPlate in the bottom level of the unit, then close door. Select SEAR CRISP, set temperature to 400°F, and set time to 15 minutes. Press the setting dial to begin preheating.
2. While unit is preheating, mix the garlic, lemon juice, oil, Za'atar, salt, and black pepper in a large bowl.
3. Coat the chops generously with the herb mixture.
4. When unit has preheated, open door, carefully remove the SearPlate with oven mitts and place on top of oven. Place the chops on the SearPlate.
5. Reinstall the SearPlate in the bottom level of the unit and close the door to begin cooking, flipping twice in between.
6. When cooking is complete, make sure lamb is cooked through with a thermometer. The internal temperature should read 145°F.
7. Remove the lamb chops the SearPlate and serve hot.

(Note: Za'atar - Za'atar is generally made with ground dried thyme, oregano, marjoram, or some combination thereof, mixed with toasted sesame seeds, and salt, though other spices such as sumac might also be added. Some commercial varieties also include roasted flour.)

Spicy Lamb Kebabs

SERVES 6

| PREP TIME: 20 minutes
| COOK TIME: 8 minutes

1 tbsp. canola oil
1 pound ground lamb
4 eggs, beaten
1 cup pistachios, chopped
4 tbsps. plain flour
4 tbsps. flat-leaf parsley, chopped
2 tsps. chili flakes
4 garlic cloves, minced
2 tbsps. fresh lemon juice
2 tsps. cumin seeds
1 tsp. fennel seeds
2 tsps. dried mint
2 tsps. salt
1 tsp. coriander seeds
1 tsp. freshly ground black pepper

1. Mix the lamb, pistachios, eggs, lemon juice, chili flakes, flour, mint, parsley, cumin seeds, fennel seeds, coriander seeds, salt and black pepper in a large bowl.
2. Thread the lamb mixture onto metal skewers to form sausages and coat with canola oil.
3. Remove Air Fry Basket from oven. Select AIR FRY, set temperature to 355°F, and set time to 8 minutes. Press the setting dial to begin preheating.
4. While unit is preheating, arrange skewers in the basket, making sure they are not crowding each other.
5. When unit has preheated, open door, install the SearPlate in the bottom level of the unit and the basket in the top level of the unit. Close door to begin cooking, flipping halfway through cooking.
6. When cooking is complete, carefully remove basket from the oven. Serve hot.

Lamb with Potatoes

SERVES 2

| PREP TIME: 20 minutes
| COOK TIME: 20 minutes

1 tsp. canola oil
½ pound lamb meat
2 small potatoes, peeled and halved
¼ cup frozen sweet potato fries

½ small onion, peeled and halved
1 garlic clove, crushed
½ tbsp. dried rosemary, crushed

1. Microwave the potatoes for about 4 minutes. Transfer the potatoes to a large bowl and stir in the canola oil and onions.
2. Rub the lamb evenly with garlic and rosemary in a medium bowl.
3. Install SearPlate in the bottom level of the unit, then close the door. Select AIR ROAST, set temperature to 375°F, and set time to 20 minutes. Press the setting dial to begin preheating.
4. When unit has preheated, open door and use oven mitts to remove SearPlate and place it on top of oven. Transfer lamb and potato mixture to the SearPlate.
5. Reinstall the SearPlate in the bottom level of the unit. Close door to begin cooking, shaking halfway through cooking.
6. When cooking is complete, carefully remove SearPlate from oven with oven mitts.
7. Serve warm.

Greek Lamb Pita Pockets

SERVES 4

| PREP TIME: 15 minutes
| COOK TIME: 6 minutes

For the Dressing:
1 cup plain yogurt
1 tbsp. lemon juice
1 tsp. dried dill weed, crushed
1 tsp. ground oregano
½ tsp. salt
For the Meatballs:
nonstick spray
½ pound (227 g) ground lamb
1 tbsp. diced onion
1 tsp. dried dill weed, crushed
1 tsp. dried parsley
¼ tsp. oregano
¼ tsp. ground cumin
¼ tsp. coriander
¼ tsp. salt
4 pita halves
For the Suggested Toppings:
1 medium cucumber, deseeded, thinly sliced
1 red onion, slivered
Crumbled Feta cheese
Sliced black olives
Chopped fresh peppers

1. Stir all the dressing ingredients together in a small bowl and refrigerate while preparing lamb.
2. Combine all the meatball ingredients in a large bowl and stir to distribute seasonings.
3. Shape the meat mixture into 12 small meatballs, rounded or slightly flattened if you prefer.
4. Remove Air Fry Basket from oven. Select AIR FRY, set temperature to 390°F, and set time to 6 minutes. Press the setting dial to begin preheating.
5. While unit is preheating, arrange meatballs in the basket, making sure they are not crowding each other. Spray with nonstick spray.
6. When unit has preheated, open door, install the SearPlate in the bottom level of the unit and the basket in the top level of the unit. Close door to begin cooking, shaking halfway through cooking.
7. When cooking is complete, carefully remove and drain on paper towels.
8. To serve, pile meatballs and the choice of toppings in pita pockets and drizzle with dressing.

Herbed Lamb Chops

SERVES 2

| PREP TIME: 10 minutes
| COOK TIME: 15 minutes

4 (4-ounces) lamb chops
1 tbsp. fresh lemon juice
1 tbsp. canola oil
1 tsp. dried rosemary
1 tsp. dried thyme

1 tsp. dried oregano
½ tsp. ground cumin
½ tsp. ground coriander
Salt and black pepper, to taste

1. Mix the oil, lemon juice, herbs, and spices in a large bowl.
2. Coat the lamb chops generously with the herb mixture and refrigerate to marinate for about 1 hour.
3. Install SearPlate in the bottom level of the unit, then close door. Select SEAR CRISP, set temperature to 390°F, and set time to 15 minutes. Press the setting dial to begin preheating.
4. When unit has preheated, open door, carefully remove the SearPlate with oven mitts and place on top of oven. Place the lamb chops on the SearPlate.
5. Reinstall the SearPlate in the bottom level of the unit and close the door to begin cooking, flipping once in between.
6. When cooking is complete, make sure lamb is cooked through with a thermometer. The internal temperature should read 145°F.
7. When cooking is complete, remove the lamb chops from the SearPlate and serve hot.

Lollipop Lamb Chops

SERVES 4

| PREP TIME: 15 minutes
| COOK TIME: 8 minutes

½ cup canola oil
8 lamb chops (1 rack)
¼ cup packed fresh parsley
¾ cup packed fresh mint
½ tsp. lemon juice
¼ cup grated Parmesan cheese
⅓ cup shelled pistachios
½ small clove garlic
¼ tsp. salt
2 tbsps. vegetable oil
Salt and freshly ground black pepper, to taste
1 tbsp. dried rosemary, chopped
1 tbsp. dried thyme

1. Prepare the pesto by combining the garlic, parsley and mint in a food processor and process until finely chopped. Add the lemon juice, Parmesan cheese, pistachios and salt. Process until all the ingredients have turned into a paste. With the processor running, slowly pour the canola oil in. Scrape the sides of the processor with a spatula and process for another 30 seconds.
2. Install SearPlate in the bottom level of the unit, then close door. Select SEAR CRISP, set temperature to 400°F, and set time to 8 minutes. Press the setting dial to begin preheating.
3. While unit is preheating, rub both sides of the lamb chops with vegetable oil and season with salt, pepper, rosemary and thyme, pressing the herbs into the meat gently with the fingers.
4. When unit has preheated, open door, carefully remove the SearPlate with oven mitts and place on top of oven. Place the lamb chops on the SearPlate.
5. Reinstall the SearPlate in the bottom level of the unit and close the door to begin cooking, flipping halfway through cooking.
6. When cooking is complete, remove the lamb chops from the SearPlate. Serve the lamb chops with mint pesto drizzled on top.

Scrumptious Lamb Chops

SERVES 4

| PREP TIME: 20 minutes
| COOK TIME: 23 minutes

3 tbsps. canola oil
4 (6-ounce) lamb chops
2 carrots, peeled and cubed
1 fennel bulb, cubed
1 parsnip, peeled and cubed
2 tbsps. fresh mint leaves, minced
1 garlic clove, minced
2 tbsps. dried rosemary
Salt and black pepper, to taste

1. Mix the herbs, garlic and oil in a large bowl and coat the lamp chops generously with this mixture.
2. Marinate in the refrigerator for about 3 hours.
3. Soak the vegetables in a large pan of water for about 15 minutes.
4. Install SearPlate in the bottom level of the unit, then close door. Select SEAR CRISP, set temperature to 390°F, and set time to 8 minutes. Press the setting dial to begin preheating.
5. When unit has preheated, open door, carefully remove the SearPlate with oven mitts and place on top of oven. Place the lamb on the SearPlate.
6. Reinstall the SearPlate in the bottom level of the unit and close the door to begin cooking.
7. After 2 minutes, open door and place the vegetables on the SearPlate. Close the door to finish cooking.
8. When cooking is complete, remove the vegetables and chops from the SearPlate. Serve warm.

Italian Lamb Chops with Avocado Mayo

SERVES 2

| PREP TIME: 5 minutes
| COOK TIME: 12 minutes

2 lamb chops
2 tsps. Italian herbs
2 avocados
½ cup mayonnaise
1 tbsp. lemon juice

1. Season the lamb chops with the Italian herbs, then set aside for 5 minutes.
2. Install SearPlate in the bottom level of the unit, then close door. Select SEAR CRISP, set temperature to 400°F, and set time to 12 minutes. Press the setting dial to begin preheating.
3. When unit has preheated, open door, carefully remove the SearPlate with oven mitts and place on top of oven. Place the lamb chops on the SearPlate.
4. Reinstall the SearPlate in the bottom level of the unit and close the door to begin cooking, flipping halfway in between.
5. Meanwhile, halve the avocados and open to remove the pits. Spoon the flesh into a blender. Pour in the mayonnaise and lemon juice and pulse until a smooth consistency is achieved.
6. When cooking is complete, make sure lamb is cooked through with a thermometer. The internal temperature should read 145°F.
7. Remove the lamb chops from the SearPlate and serve with the avocado mayo.

CHAPTER 8
BEEF

Avocado Buttered Flank Steak

SERVES 1

| PREP TIME: 5 minutes
| COOK TIME: 12 minutes

1 flank steak
Salt and ground black pepper, to taste
2 avocados
2 tbsps. clarified butter
½ cup chimichurri sauce

1. Rub the flank steak with salt and pepper to taste and let sit for 20 minutes.
2. Install SearPlate in the bottom level of the unit, then close door. Select SEAR CRISP, set temperature to 400°F, and set time to 12 minutes. Press the setting dial to begin preheating.
3. When unit has preheated, open door, carefully remove the SearPlate with oven mitts and place on top of oven. Place the flank steak on the SearPlate.
4. Reinstall the SearPlate in the bottom level of the unit and close the door to begin cooking, flipping halfway through cooking.
5. Meanwhile, halve the avocados and take out the pits. Spoon the flesh into a medium bowl and mash with a fork. Mix in the clarified butter and chimichurri sauce, making sure everything is well combined.
6. After 12 minutes, begin to check steak for doneness. If further doneness is desired, leave in oven.
7. When cooking is complete, remove the steak from the SearPlate. Serve the steak with the avocado butter.

Beef and Mushroom Meatloaf

SERVES 4

| PREP TIME: 15 minutes
| COOK TIME: 25 minutes

1 tbsp. canola oil
1 pound lean ground beef
1 egg, lightly beaten
1 small onion, finely chopped
3 tbsps. dry breadcrumbs
2 mushrooms, thickly sliced
Salt and ground black pepper, as required

1. Mix the beef, onion, canola oil, breadcrumbs, egg, salt, and black pepper in a bowl until well combined.
2. Transfer the mixture into a greased loaf pan and top with mushroom slices.
3. Install rack in bottom position, then close door. Select BAKE, set temperature to 390°F, and set time to 25 minutes. Press the setting dial to begin preheating.
4. When unit has preheated, open door and place pan onto the center of the rack. Close door to begin cooking.
5. When cooking is complete, carefully remove pan from the oven. Cut into desired size wedges and serve warm.

Roasted Beef Ribs

SERVES 4

| PREP TIME: 20 minutes
| COOK TIME: 8 minutes

½ cup canola oil
1 pound (454 g) meaty beef ribs, rinsed and drained
1 cup coriander, finely chopped
3 tbsps. apple cider vinegar
1 tbsp. fresh basil leaves, chopped
2 garlic cloves, finely chopped
1 chipotle powder
1 tsp. fennel seeds
1 tsp. hot paprika
Kosher salt and black pepper, to taste

1. Coat the beef ribs with the remaining ingredients and refrigerate for at least 3 hours.
2. Install SearPlate in the bottom level of the unit, then close the door. Select AIR ROAST, set temperature to 390°F, and set time to 8 minutes. Press the setting dial to begin preheating.
3. When unit has preheated, open door and use oven mitts to remove SearPlate and place it on top of oven. Separate the ribs from the marinade and transfer to the SearPlate.
4. Reinstall the SearPlate in the bottom level of the unit. Close door to begin cooking, flipping halfway through cooking.
5. After 8 minutes, begin to check ribs for doneness. If further doneness is desired, leave in oven.
6. When cooking is complete, carefully remove SearPlate from oven with oven mitts. Pour the remaining marinade over the ribs before serving.

Perfect Skirt Steak

SERVES 2

| PREP TIME: 15 minutes
| COOK TIME: 8 minutes

2 (8-ounce) skirt steaks
1 cup fresh parsley leaves, chopped finely
¾ cup canola oil
3 tbsps. fresh oregano, chopped finely
3 tbsps. fresh mint leaves, chopped finely
3 garlic cloves, minced
1 tbsp. ground cumin
2 tsps. smoked paprika
1 tsp. cayenne pepper
1 tsp. red pepper flakes, crushed
Salt and freshly ground black pepper, to taste
3 tbsps. red wine vinegar

1. Season the steaks with a little salt and black pepper.
2. Combine all the ingredients in a large bowl except the steaks.
3. Put ¼ cup of the herb mixture and steaks in a resealable bag and shake well.
4. Refrigerate for about 24 hours and reserve the remaining herb mixture.
5. Keep the steaks at room temperature for about 30 minutes.
6. Install SearPlate in the bottom level of the unit, then close door. Select SEAR CRISP, set temperature to 425°F, and set time to 8 minutes. Press the setting dial to begin preheating.
7. When unit has preheated, open door, carefully remove the SearPlate with oven mitts and place on top of oven. Place the steaks on the SearPlate.
8. Reinstall the SearPlate in the bottom level of the unit and close the door to begin cooking, flipping halfway. After 8 minutes, begin to check steak for doneness. If further doneness is desired, leave in oven.
9. When cooking is complete, remove the steaks from the SearPlate and sprinkle with remaining herb mixture to serve.

Crispy Sirloin Steak

SERVES 2

| PREP TIME: 15 minutes
| COOK TIME: 10 minutes

nonstick spray
1 cup white flour
2 eggs
2 (6-ounces) sirloin steaks, pounded
1 cup panko breadcrumbs
1 tsp. onion powder
1 tsp. garlic powder
Salt and black pepper, to taste

1. Place the flour in a shallow bowl and whisk eggs in a second dish.
2. Mix the panko breadcrumbs and spices in a third bowl.
3. Rub the steaks with flour, dip into the eggs and coat with breadcrumb mixture.
4. Remove Air Fry Basket from oven. Select AIR FRY, set temperature to 360°F, and set time to 10 minutes. Press the setting dial to begin preheating.
5. While unit is preheating, arrange steaks in the basket, making sure they are not crowding each other. Spray with nonstick spray.
6. When unit has preheated, open door, install the SearPlate in the bottom level of the unit and the basket in the top level of the unit. Close door to begin cooking, flipping halfway through cooking.
7. When cooking is complete, carefully remove basket from the oven. Transfer the steaks to a plate and cut into desired size slices to serve.

Simple Striploin Steak

SERVES 2

| PREP TIME: 10 minutes
| COOK TIME: 8 minutes

2 (7-ounces) striploin steaks
1½ tbsps. coconut butter
Salt and black pepper, to taste

1. Install SearPlate in the bottom level of the unit, then close door. Select SEAR CRISP, set temperature to 425°F, and set time to 8 minutes. Press the setting dial to begin preheating.
2. While unit is preheating, rub the steaks generously with salt and black pepper and coat with butter.
3. When unit has preheated, open door, carefully remove the SearPlate with oven mitts and place on top of oven. Place the steaks on the SearPlate.
4. Reinstall the SearPlate in the bottom level of the unit and close the door to begin cooking, flipping once in between.
5. After 8 minutes, begin to check steak for doneness. If further doneness is desired, leave in oven.
6. When cooking is complete, remove the steaks from the SearPlate and cut into desired size slices to serve.

Swedish Beef Meatballs

SERVES 8

| PREP TIME: 10 minutes
| COOK TIME: 11 minutes

cooking spray
1 pound (454 g) ground beef
2 carrots, shredded
1 egg, beaten
2 whole wheat bread slices, crumbled
1 small onion, minced
2 cups pasta sauce
1 cup tomato sauce
½ tsp. garlic salt
Pepper and salt, to taste

1. In a medium bowl, combine the ground beef, egg, carrots, crumbled bread, onion, garlic salt, pepper and salt to taste.
2. Divide the mixture into equal amounts and shape each one into a small meatball.
3. Install SearPlate in the bottom level of the unit, then close the door. Select AIR ROAST, set temperature to 400°F, and set time to 11 minutes. Press the setting dial to begin preheating.
4. When unit has preheated, open door and use oven mitts to remove SearPlate and place it on top of oven. Transfer meatballs to the SearPlate. Spray with cooking spray.
5. Reinstall the SearPlate in the bottom level of the unit. Close door to begin cooking.
6. After 7 minutes, open door and top with the tomato sauce and pasta sauce. Close door to finish cooking.
7. When cooking is complete, carefully remove SearPlate from oven with oven mitts. Serve hot.

Ribeye Steak with Peanut Butter

SERVES 1

| PREP TIME: 5 minutes
| COOK TIME: 10 minutes

1 tbsp. peanut oil
1 (1-pound / 454-g) ribeye steak
Salt and ground black pepper, to taste
½ tbsp. peanut butter
½ tsp. thyme, chopped

1. Install SearPlate in the bottom level of the unit, then close door. Select SEAR CRISP, set temperature to 400°F, and set time to 10 minutes. Press the setting dial to begin preheating.
2. While unit is preheating, Season the steak with salt and pepper. Drizzle with the peanut oil.
3. When unit has preheated, open door, carefully remove the SearPlate with oven mitts and place on top of oven. Place the steak on the SearPlate.
4. Reinstall the SearPlate in the bottom level of the unit and close the door to begin cooking.
5. After 8 minutes, open door and toss in butter and thyme. Close door to finish cooking. Check steak for doneness. If further doneness is desired, leave in oven.
6. When cooking is complete, remove the steak from the SearPlate. Rest for 5 minutes and serve.

Classic Skirt Steak Strips with Veggies

SERVES 4

| PREP TIME: 10 minutes
| COOK TIME: 10 minutes

1 (12-ounce) skirt steak, cut into thin strips
6-ounce snow peas
½ pound fresh mushrooms, quartered
1 onion, cut into half rings
¼ cup canola oil, divided
2 tbsps. honey
2 tbsps. soy sauce
Salt and black pepper, to taste

1. Install SearPlate in the bottom level of the unit, then close door. Select SEAR CRISP, set temperature to 425°F, and set time to 10 minutes. Press the setting dial to begin preheating.
2. While unit is preheating, mix 2 tbsps. of oil, soy sauce and honey in a medium bowl and coat the steak strips with this marinade.
3. Put the vegetables, remaining oil, salt and black pepper in another bowl and toss well.
4. When unit has preheated, open door, carefully remove the SearPlate with oven mitts and place on top of oven. Place the steak strips on the left side and vegetables on the right.
5. Reinstall the SearPlate in the bottom level of the unit and close the door to begin cooking.
6. When cooking is complete, remove the steak strips and vegetables from the SearPlate and and serve warm.

Flank Steak with Soy Sauce

SERVES 4

| PREP TIME: 10 minutes
| COOK TIME: 10 minutes

cooking spray
2 tsp. vegetable oil
1 pound flank steaks, sliced
½ cup soy sauce
¼ cup xanthum gum
¾ cup swerve, packed
½ tsp. ginger
1 tbsp. garlic, minced
½ cup water

1. Install SearPlate in the bottom level of the unit, then close door. Select SEAR CRISP, set temperature to 390°F, and set time to 10 minutes. Press the setting dial to begin preheating.
2. While unit is preheating, coat the steaks with xanthum gum on both the sides and spray with cooking spray.
3. When unit has preheated, open door, carefully remove the SearPlate with oven mitts and place on top of oven. Place the steaks on the SearPlate.
4. Reinstall the SearPlate in the bottom level of the unit and close the door to begin cooking, flipping halfway through cooking. After 10 minutes, begin to check steak for doneness. If further doneness is desired, leave in oven.
5. When cooking is complete, remove the steaks to a plate and cut to desired slices.
6. Cook the rest of the ingredients for the sauce in a saucepan. Bring to a boil and pour over the steak slices to serve.

CHAPTER 9
SNACK

Cheese Filled Bell Peppers

SERVES 3

| PREP TIME: 15 minutes
| COOK TIME: 12 minutes

cooking spray
1 small green bell pepper
1 small red bell pepper
1 small yellow bell pepper
½ cup mozzarella cheese
½ cup cream cheese
3 tsps. red chili flakes

1. Chop the tops of the bell peppers and remove all the seeds.
2. Mix together mozzarella cheese, cream cheese and red chili flakes in a medium bowl.
3. Stuff this cheese mixture in the bell peppers and put back the tops.
4. Install SearPlate in the bottom level of the unit, then close the door. Select AIR ROAST, set temperature to 320°F, and set time to 12 minutes. Press the setting dial to begin preheating.
5. When unit has preheated, open door and use oven mitts to remove SearPlate and place it on top of oven. Transfer bell peppers to the SearPlate and spray with cooking spray.
6. Reinstall the SearPlate in the bottom level of the unit. Close door to begin cooking, flipping halfway through cooking.
7. When cooking is complete, carefully remove SearPlate from oven with oven mitts. Serve hot.

Fast and Easy Tortilla Chips

SERVES 2

| PREP TIME: 5 minutes
| COOK TIME: 6 minutes

8 corn tortillas
1 tbsp. canola oil
Salt, to taste

1. Remove Air Fry Basket from oven. Select AIR FRY, set temperature to 390°F, and set time to 25 minutes. Press the setting dial to begin preheating.
2. While unit is preheating, slice the corn tortillas into triangles. Coat with a light brushing of canola oil.
3. Arrange half of the corn tortillas in the basket, making sure they are not crowding each other.
4. When unit has preheated, open door, install the SearPlate in the bottom level of the unit and the basket in the top level of the unit. Close door to begin cooking, flipping halfway through cooking.
5. Repeat with the remaining tortilla pieces.
6. When cooking is complete, carefully remove basket from the oven. Season with salt before serving.

Spiced Sweet Potato Fries

SERVES 2

| PREP TIME: 10 minutes
| COOK TIME: 25 minutes

2 tbsps. canola oil
2 medium sweet potatoes (about 10 ounces / 284 g each), cut into wedges, ½ inch thick and 3 inches long
1½ tsps. kosher salt, plus more as needed
1½ tsps. smoked paprika
1 tsp. chili powder
½ tsp. ground cumin
½ tsp. ground turmeric
½ tsp. mustard powder
¼ tsp. cayenne pepper
Freshly ground black pepper, to taste
⅔ cup sour cream
1 garlic clove, grated

1. Remove Air Fry Basket from oven. Select AIR FRY, set temperature to 400°F, and set time to 25 minutes. Press the setting dial to begin preheating.
2. While unit is preheating, combine the canola oil, paprika, salt, chili powder, cumin, turmeric, mustard powder, and cayenne in a large bowl.
3. Add the sweet potatoes, season with black pepper, and toss to evenly coat.
4. Place the sweet potatoes in the basket, making sure they are not crowding each other.
5. When unit has preheated, open door, install the SearPlate in the bottom level of the unit and the basket in the top level of the unit. Close door to begin cooking, shaking halfway through cooking.
6. Meanwhile, stir together the sour cream and garlic in a small bowl. Season with salt and black pepper and transfer to a serving dish.
7. When cooking is complete, carefully remove basket from the oven. Serve the potato wedges hot with the garlic sour cream.

Coconut-Crusted Shrimp

SERVES 2-4

| PREP TIME: 10 minutes
| COOK TIME: 4 minutes

Cooking spray
½ pound (227 g) medium shrimp, peeled and deveined (tails intact)
1 cup canned coconut milk
1 cup coconut yogurt
½ cup panko bread crumbs
½ cup unsweetened shredded coconut
Finely grated zest of 1 lime
Kosher salt, to taste
Freshly ground black pepper, to taste
1 small or ½ medium cucumber, halved and deseeded
1 serrano chile, deseeded and minced

1. In a bowl, combine the shrimp, coconut milk, lime zest, and ½ tsp. kosher salt. Let the shrimp sit for about 10 minutes.
2. Meanwhile, in a separate bowl, stir together the bread crumbs and shredded coconut and season with salt and pepper to taste.
3. A few at a time, add the shrimp to the bread crumb mixture and toss to coat completely. Transfer the shrimp to a wire rack set over a baking sheet. Spray the shrimp all over with cooking spray.
4. Remove Air Fry Basket from oven. Select AIR FRY, set temperature to 400°F, and set time to 4 minutes. Press the setting dial to begin preheating.
5. While unit is preheating, arrange shrimp in the basket, making sure they are not crowding each other.
6. When unit has preheated, open door, install the SearPlate in the bottom level of the unit and the basket in the top level of the unit. Close door to begin cooking, flipping halfway through cooking.
7. When cooking is complete, carefully remove basket from the oven. Transfer the shrimp to a serving platter and season with more salt.
8. Grate the cucumber into a small bowl. Stir in the coconut yogurt and chile and season with salt and pepper. Serve the shrimp with the chile yogurt.

Party Time Mixed Nuts

SERVES 3

| PREP TIME: 15 minutes
| COOK TIME: 14 minutes

nonstick spray
1 tbsp. canola oil
½ cup raw peanuts
½ cup raisins
½ cup raw almonds
½ cup raw cashew nuts
½ cup pecans
Salt, to taste

1. Remove Air Fry Basket from oven. Select AIR FRY, set temperature to 320°F, and set time to 14 minutes. Press the setting dial to begin preheating.
2. While unit is preheating, arrange nuts in the basket, making sure they are not crowding each other. Spray with non-stick spray.
3. When unit has preheated, open door, install the SearPlate in the bottom level of the unit and the basket in the top level of the unit. Close door to begin cooking.
4. After 9 minutes, open door, drizzle with canola oil and toss to coat well. Close door to finish cooking.
5. When cooking is complete, carefully remove basket from the oven. Serve warm.

Cheesy Apple Roll-Ups

MAKES 8 ROLL-UPS

| PREP TIME: 5 minutes
| COOK TIME: 5 minutes

8 slices whole wheat sandwich bread
½ small apple, chopped
4 ounces (113 g) Colby Jack cheese, grated
2 tbsps. coconut butter, melted

1. Install SearPlate in the bottom level of the unit, then close the door. Select RAPID BAKE, set temperature to 390°F, and set the time to 5 minutes.
2. While unit is preheating, remove the crusts from the bread and flatten the slices with a rolling pin. Don't be gentle. Press hard so that bread will be very thin.
3. Top the bread slices with cheese and chopped apple, dividing the ingredients evenly.
4. Roll up each slice tightly and secure each with one or two toothpicks.
5. Brush outside of rolls with melted coconut butter.
6. When unit has preheated, open the door, carefully remove the SearPlate with oven mitts, and place on top of the oven. Carefully place rolls on the SearPlate. Reinstall the SearPlate in the bottom level of the unit and close the door to begin cooking, until outside is crisp and nicely browned.
7. When cooking is complete, remove SearPlate and set aside to cool for 5 minutes. Serve hot.

Crispy Potato Chips

SERVES 6

| PREP TIME: 15 minutes
| COOK TIME: 30 minutes

nonstick spray
4 small russet potatoes, thinly sliced
2 tbsps. fresh rosemary, finely chopped
1 tbsp. canola oil
¼ tsp. salt

1. Remove Air Fry Basket from oven. Select AIR FRY, set temperature to 400°F, and set time to 30 minutes. Press the setting dial to begin preheating.
2. While unit is preheating, mix together the potato slices, canola oil, rosemary and salt in a large bowl.
3. Arrange potato slices in the basket, making sure they are not crowding each other. Spray with nonstick spray.
4. When unit has preheated, open door, install the SearPlate in the bottom level of the unit and the basket in the top level of the unit. Close door to begin cooking, flipping halfway through cooking.
5. When cooking is complete, carefully remove basket from the oven. Serve warm.

Spicy Jacket Potatoes

SERVES 2

| PREP TIME: 15 minutes
| COOK TIME: 20 minutes

cooking spray
2 potatoes
3 tbsps. sour cream
¼ cup tomatoes, chopped
1 tbsp. parmesan cheese, shredded
1 tbsp. butter, softened
1 tsp. parsley, minced
Salt and black pepper, to taste

1. Install SearPlate in the bottom level of the unit, then close the door. Select AIR ROAST, set temperature to 355°F, and set time to 20 minutes. Press the setting dial to begin preheating.
2. While unit is preheating, make holes in the potatoes and spray with cooking spray.
3. When unit has preheated, open door and use oven mitts to remove SearPlate and place it on top of oven. Transfer potatoes to the SearPlate.
4. Reinstall the SearPlate in the bottom level of the unit. Close door to begin cooking, flipping halfway through cooking.
5. Meanwhile, mix together the remaining ingredients in a bowl and combine well.
6. When cooking is complete, carefully remove SearPlate from oven with oven mitts. Cut the potatoes from the center and stuff in the cheese mixture to serve.

Buttered Corn on the Cob

SERVES 2

| PREP TIME: 15 minutes
| COOK TIME: 20 minutes

2 corn on the cob
2 tbsps. coconut butter, softened and divided
Salt and black pepper, to taste

1. Install SearPlate in the bottom level of the unit, then close the door. Select AIR ROAST, set temperature to 400°F, and set time to 20 minutes. Press the setting dial to begin preheating.
2. While unit is preheating, season the cobs evenly with salt and black pepper and rub with 1 tbsp. butter. Wrap the cobs in foil paper.
3. When unit has preheated, open door and use oven mitts to remove SearPlate and place it on top of oven. Transfer the cobs to the SearPlate.
4. Reinstall the SearPlate in the bottom level of the unit. Close door to begin cooking.
5. When cooking is complete, carefully remove SearPlate from oven with oven mitts. Top with remaining butter and serve warm.

Mozzarella Arancini

MAKES 16 ARANCINI

| PREP TIME: 5 minutes
| COOK TIME: 20 minutes

nonstick spray
2 tbsps. canola oil
2 cups cooked rice, cooled
1½ cups panko bread crumbs, divided
2 eggs, beaten
½ cup grated Parmesan cheese
2 tbsps. minced fresh basil
16 (¾-inch) cubes Mozzarella cheese

1. In a medium bowl, combine the rice, eggs, ½ cup of the bread crumbs, Parmesan cheese and basil. Form this mixture into 16 1½-inch balls.
2. Poke a hole in each of the balls with your finger and insert a Mozzarella cube. Form the rice mixture firmly around the cheese.
3. On a shallow plate, mix the remaining 1 cup of the bread crumbs with the canola oil and combine well. Roll the rice balls in the bread crumbs to coat.
4. Remove Air Fry Basket from oven. Select AIR FRY, set temperature to 400°F, and set time to 10 minutes. Press the setting dial to begin preheating.
5. While unit is preheating, arrange half of the arancini in the basket, making sure they are not crowding each other. Spray with nonstick spray.
6. When unit has preheated, open door, install the SearPlate in the bottom level of the unit and the basket in the top level of the unit. Close door to begin cooking, until golden brown.
7. Repeat with the remaining arancini.
8. When cooking is complete, carefully remove basket from the oven. Serve hot.

CHAPTER 10
DESSERT

Dark Chocolate Cake

SERVES 4

| PREP TIME: 10 minutes
| COOK TIME: 13 minutes

cooking spray
1½ tbsps. almond flour
2 eggs
3½ oz. sugar free dark chocolate, chopped
3½ oz. peanut butter
3½ tbsps. swerve

1. Spray 4 regular sized ramekins with cooking spray.
2. Microwave all chocolate bits with peanut butter in a bowl for about 3 minutes.
3. Remove from the microwave and whisk in the eggs and swerve.
4. Stir in the flour and combine well until smooth. Transfer the mixture into the ramekins.
5. Install rack in bottom position, then close door. Select BAKE, set temperature to 375°F, and set time to 10 minutes. Press the setting dial to begin preheating.
6. When unit has preheated, open door and place ramekins onto the center of the rack. Close door to begin cooking.
7. After 10 minutes, check cakes for doneness by sticking a toothpick in the center of the cakes. If it comes out clean, remove from oven.
8. When cooking is complete, carefully remove ramekins from the oven. Serve hot.

Chocolate Soufflé

SERVES 2

| PREP TIME: 15 minutes
| COOK TIME: 16 minutes

cooking spray
3 ounces semi-sweet chocolate, chopped
2 eggs, egg yolks and whites separated
¼ cup butter
3 tbsps. sugar
2 tbsps. all-purpose flour
½ tsp. pure vanilla extract
1 tsp. powdered sugar plus extra for dusting

1. Spray 2 ramekins with cooking spray.
2. Microwave the butter and chocolate on high heat for about 2 minutes until smooth.
3. Whisk the egg yolks, sugar, and vanilla extract in a medium bowl.
4. Add the chocolate mixture and flour and mix until well combined.
5. Whisk the egg whites in another bowl until soft peaks form and fold into the chocolate mixture.
6. Sprinkle each with a pinch of sugar and transfer the mixture into the ramekins.
7. Install rack in bottom position, then close door. Select BAKE, set temperature to 330°F, and set time to 14 minutes. Press the setting dial to begin preheating.
8. When unit has preheated, open door and place ramekins onto the center of the rack. Close door to begin cooking.
9. When cooking is complete, carefully remove ramekins from the oven. Serve sprinkled with the powdered sugar to serve.

Oatmeal and Carrot Cookie Cups

MAKES 16 CUPS

| PREP TIME: 10 minutes
| COOK TIME: 8 minutes

3 tbsps. unsalted butter, at room temperature
¼ cup packed brown sugar
1 egg white
½ cup quick-cooking oatmeal
⅓ cup finely grated carrot
⅓ cup whole-wheat pastry flour
¼ cup dried cherries
1 tbsp. honey
½ tsp. vanilla extract
½ tsp. baking soda

1. In a medium bowl, beat the butter, brown sugar and honey until well combined.
2. Add the egg white, vanilla and carrot. Beat to combine well.
3. Stir in the oatmeal, pastry flour and baking soda. Stir in the dried cherries.
4. Double up 32 mini muffin foil cups to make 16 cups. Fill each with about 4 tsps. of dough.
5. Place 8 muffin cups in a baking pan.
6. Install rack in bottom position, then close door. Select BAKE, set temperature to 350°F, and set time to 8 minutes. Press the setting dial to begin preheating.
7. When unit has preheated, open door and place pan onto the center of the rack. Close door to begin cooking, until light golden brown and just set.
8. Repeat with the remaining muffin cups.
9. When cooking is complete, carefully remove pan from the oven. Serve warm.

Avocado Walnut Bread

SERVES 6

| PREP TIME: 5 minutes
| COOK TIME: 35 minutes

2 tbsps. canola oil
¾ cup (3 oz.) almond flour, white
2 ripe avocados, cored, peeled and mashed
2 large eggs, beaten
½ cup granulated swerve
¼ tsp. baking soda
2 tbsps. (¾ oz.) Toasted walnuts, chopped roughly
1 tsp. cinnamon ground
½ tsp. kosher salt
1 tsp. vanilla extract

1. Line a 6-inch baking pan with parchment paper.
2. Mix the almond flour, salt, baking soda, and cinnamon in a small bowl.
3. Whisk the eggs with avocado mash, yogurt, swerve, oil, and vanilla in a medium bowl.
4. Stir in the almond flour mixture and mix until well combined.
5. Pour the batter evenly into the pan and top with the walnuts.
6. Install rack in bottom position, then close door. Select BAKE, set temperature to 310°F, and set time to 35 minutes. Press the setting dial to begin preheating.
7. When unit has preheated, open door and place pan onto the center of the rack. Close door to begin cooking.
8. After 35 minutes, check bread for doneness by sticking a toothpick in the center of the bread. If it comes out clean, remove from oven.
9. When cooking is complete, carefully remove pan from the oven. Cut the bread into slices and serve.

Walnut Banana Cake

SERVES 6

| PREP TIME: 5 minutes
| COOK TIME: 40 minutes

cooking spray
½ cup canola oil
1½ cups cake flour
3 medium bananas, peeled and mashed
½ cup walnuts, chopped
2 eggs
½ cup coconut sugar
1 tsp. baking soda
½ tsp. ground cinnamon
½ tsp. vanilla extract
Salt, to taste

1. Spray a 6-inch round baking pan lightly with cooking spray.
2. Mix the flour, baking soda, cinnamon and salt in a bowl until well combined.
3. Whisk the egg with canola oil, vanilla extract, sugar and bananas in another bowl.
4. Stir in the flour mixture slowly until well combined. Gently fold in the chopped walnuts.
5. Pour the mixture into the baking pan and spread evenly. Cover with the foil paper.
6. Install rack in bottom position, then close door. Select BAKE, set temperature to 300°F, and set time to 40 minutes. Press the setting dial to begin preheating.
7. When unit has preheated, open door and place pan onto the center of the rack. Close door to begin cooking.
8. After 30 minutes, open door and remove the foil. Close door to finish cooking.
9. When cooking is complete, carefully remove pan from the oven. Cut the bread into slices to serve.

Cardamom and Vanilla Custard

SERVES 2

| PREP TIME: 5 minutes
| COOK TIME: 25 minutes

2 tbsps. plus 1 tsp. sugar
1 cup whole milk
1 large egg
¼ tsp. vanilla bean paste or pure vanilla extract
¼ tsp. ground cardamom, plus more for sprinkling

1. Install rack in bottom position, then close door. Select BAKE, set temperature to 350°F, and set time to 25 minutes. Press the setting dial to begin preheating.
2. While unit is preheating, beat together the milk, egg, sugar, vanilla, and cardamom in a medium bowl.
3. Divide the mixture between the ramekins. Sprinkle lightly with cardamom. Cover each ramekin tightly with aluminum foil.
4. When unit has preheated, open door and place ramekins onto the center of the rack. Close door to begin cooking, until a toothpick inserted in the center comes out clean.
5. When cooking is complete, carefully remove ramekins from the oven. Let the custards cool on a wire rack for 5 to 10 minutes. Serve warm.

Basic Butter Cookies

SERVES 8

| PREP TIME: 10 minutes
| COOK TIME: 10 minutes

cooking spray
4-ounce unsalted butter
1¼-ounce icing sugar
1 cup all-purpose flour
¼ tsp. baking powder

1. Spray a baking sheet lightly with cooking spray.
2. Mix the butter, icing sugar, flour and baking powder in a large bowl.
3. Mix well until a dough is formed and transfer into the piping bag fitted with a fluted nozzle.
4. Pipe the dough onto the baking sheet.
5. Install rack in bottom position, then close door. Select BAKE, set temperature to 340°F, and set time to 10 minutes. Press the setting dial to begin preheating.
6. When unit has preheated, open door and place sheet onto the center of the rack. Close door to begin cooking, until golden brown.
7. When cooking is complete, carefully remove sheet from the oven. Serve with tea.

Strawberry Cupcakes

SERVES 8

| PREP TIME: 10 minutes
| COOK TIME: 8 minutes

For the Cupcakes:
cooking spray
7 tbsps. butter
2 eggs
7/8 cup self-rising flour
½ cup caster sugar
½ tsp. vanilla essence
For the Icing:
3½ tbsps. butter
¼ cup fresh strawberries, blended
1 cup icing sugar
1 tbsp. whipped cream
½ tsp. pink food color

1. Grease 8 muffin tins lightly with cooking spray.
2. Mix all the cupcakes ingredients in a large bowl until well combined.
3. Pour the mixture into muffin tins. Place the muffin tins on a baking pan.
4. Install rack in bottom position, then close door. Select BAKE, set temperature to 340°F, and set time to 8 minutes. Press the setting dial to begin preheating.
5. When unit has preheated, open door and place pan onto the center of the rack. Close door to begin cooking.
6. Meanwhile, mix all the icing ingredients in a large bowl until well combined.
7. After 8 minutes, check cupcakes for doneness by sticking a toothpick in the center of the cupcakes. If it comes out clean, remove from oven.
8. When cooking is complete, carefully remove pan from the oven. Fill the pastry bag with icing and top each cupcake evenly with frosting to serve.

Decadent Cheesecake

SERVES 6

| PREP TIME: 15 minutes
| COOK TIME: 33 minutes

cooking spray
3 eggs, separated
1 cup white chocolate, chopped
½ cup cream cheese, softened
¼ cup apricot jam
2 tbsps. cocoa powder
2 tbsps. powdered sugar

1. Spray a cake pan lightly with cooking spray.
2. Refrigerate the egg whites in a bowl to chill before using.
3. Microwave the chocolate and cream cheese on high for about 3 minutes.
4. Remove from the microwave and whisk in the egg yolks.
5. Whisk together egg whites until firm peaks form and combine with the chocolate mixture and cocoa powder.
6. Transfer the mixture into the cake pan.
7. Install rack in bottom position, then close door. Select BAKE, set temperature to 285°F, and set time to 30 minutes. Press the setting dial to begin preheating.
8. When unit has preheated, open door and place the cake pan onto the center of the rack. Close door to begin cooking.
9. When cooking is complete, carefully remove pan from the oven. Dust with powdered sugar and spread jam on top to serve.

Honey-Roasted Pears

SERVES 4

| PREP TIME: 5 minutes
| COOK TIME: 20 minutes

2 large Bosc pears, halved and deseeded
¼ cup walnuts, chopped
¼ cup part skim low-fat ricotta cheese, divided
3 tbsps. honey
1 tbsp. unsalted butter
½ tsp. ground cinnamon

1. In a baking pan, arrange the pears, cut side up.
2. In a small microwave-safe bowl, melt the honey, butter, and cinnamon. Brush this mixture over the cut sides of the pears.
3. Pour 3 tbsps. of water around the pears in the pan.
4. Install rack in bottom position and close the door. Select AIR ROAST, set temperature to 350°F, and set time to 20 minutes. Press the setting dial to begin preheating.
5. When unit is preheated, open the door and place the pan onto the center of the rack. Close door to begin cooking, until tender when pierced with a fork and slightly crisp on the edges, basting once with the liquid in the pan.
6. When cooking is complete, carefully remove the pears from the pan and place on a serving plate. Drizzle each with some liquid from the pan, sprinkle the walnuts on top, and serve with a spoonful of ricotta cheese.

APPENDIX 1: NINJA FOODI DUAL HEAT AIR FRYER OVEN TIMETABLE

RAPID BAKE CHART

INGREDIENT	AMOUNT	PREPARATION	TEMP	TIME
Premade cinnamon rolls (refrigerated)	1 tube (8 rolls)	Follow directions on package	Recommended Temp on package	10-13 mins
Store-bought chocolate chip cookie dough	1 package (12 cookies)	Follow directions on package	Recommended Temp on package	6-8 mins
Store-bought sugar cookie dough	1 package (12 cookies)	Follow directions on package	Recommended Temp on package	7-9 mins
Store-bought biscuits (refrigerated)	1 tube (8 biscuits)	Follow directions on package	Recommended Temp on package	9-11 mins
Boxed coffee cake mix	1 box	Follow directions on package	Recommended Temp on package	20-22 mins
Crescent rolls (refrigerated)	1 tube (8 rolls)	Follow directions on package	Recommended Temp on package	6-9 mins
9-inch apple pie (frozen)	1 pie	N/A	Reduce recommended Temp on package by 25°F	28-32 mins
Boxed cornbread mix	1 box	Follow directions on package	Reduce recommended Temp on package by 25°F	15-20 mins
Boxed brownie mix	1 box	Follow directions on package	Reduce recommended Temp on package by 25°F	20-25 mins
Boxed banana bread mix	1 box	Follow directions on package	Reduce recommended Temp on package by 25°F	40-45 mins
Individual frozen pot pie	1 pie	N/A	Reduce recommended Temp on package by 25°F	15-25 mins
Family-sized frozen pot pie	1 pie	N/A	Reduce recommended Temp on package by 25°F	30-40 mins
Dinner rolls (frozen)	8 rolls	N/A	Recommended Temp on package	5-8 mins
Puff pastry shells (frozen)	6 shells	N/A	Recommended Temp on package	8-12 mins
Turnovers (frozen)	4 turnovers	N/A	Recommended Temp on package	10-14 mins
Sandwich pockets (frozen)	2 pockets	N/A	Recommended Temp on package	18-20 mins

AIR FRY COOKING CHART

INGREDIENT	AMOUNT	PREPARATION	TEMP	TIME
FROZEN FOOD				
Chicken nuggets	2 boxes (24 oz)	None	400°F	26-30 mins
Chicken thighs	8 thighs (8-10 oz each)	None	390°F	26-30 mins
Chicken wings	2 lbs	None	400°F	24-28 mins
Egg Rolls	Up to 2 lbs	None	360°F	18-20 mins
Fish fillets	1 package (10 fillets)	None	400°F	16-18 mins
Fish sticks	1 box (16 oz)	None	400°F	14-16 mins
French fries	16 oz	None	390°F	22-24 mins
Mozzarella sticks	Up to 2 lbs	None	375°F	10-15 mins
Pizza Rolls	Up to 2 lbs	None	375°F	10-13 mins
Popcorn shrimp	Up to 2 lbs	None	390°F	10-11 mins
Pot stickers	3 bag (30 count)	None	390°F	14-18 mins
Tater tots	2 lbs	None	360°F	20-25 mins
MEAT, POULTRY, FISH				
Bacon	½ package (8 oz)	None	390°F	7-10 mins
Burgers	5 ¼-lb patties, 80% lean	1 inch thick	375°F	10-12 mins
Chicken drumsticks	6 drumsticks	Pat dry	400°F	22-35 mins
Chicken thighs,bone in, skin on	5 thighs (4-6 oz each)	Pat dry	390°F	22-28 mins
Chicken wings	2 lbs	Pat dry	400°F	28-30 mins
Crab cakes	8 cakes (6-8 oz each)	None	400°F	12-17 mins
Salmon fillets	6-8 fillets (6-8 oz each)	None	400°F	15-20 mins
Sausages	10 sausages (3 oz each)	None	390°F	15-20 mins
Shrimp, peeled	2 lbs	Pat dry	390°F	7-10 mins
VEGETABLES				
Asparagus	Up to 2 lbs	Trim stems	400°F	8-10 mins
Beets	1.5 lbs	Peel, cut in ½-inch cubes	390°F	28-30 mins
Bell peppers (for roasting)	4 peppers	Cut in quarters, remove seeds	425°F	15-20 mins
Broccoli	Up to 2 lbs	Cut in 1-2-inch florets	375°F	15-17 mins
Carrots	1 lb	Peel, cut in ¼-inch rounds	425°F	15-20 mins
Cauliflower	Up to 2 lbs	Cut in 1-2-inch florets	390°F	15-18 mins
Corn on the cob	7 ears	Whole ears, remove husks	400°F	14-17 mins
Green beans	Up to 2 lbs	Stems trimmed	425°F	10-12 mins
Kale (for chips)	4 oz	Tear into pieces, remove stem	325°F	8-10 mins
Mushrooms	16 oz	Rinse, slice thinly	390°F	20-25 mins
Potato Wedges	Up to 2 lbs	Cut in 1-inch wedges	390°F	28-31 mins
Potatoes, russet	1 lb	Hand-cut fries, soak 20 mins in cold water, then pat dry	410°F	25-30 mins
Potatoes, sweet	1 lb	Hand-cut fries, soak 30 mins in cold water, then pat dry	400°F	25-28 mins
Yellow Squash	2 lbs	Cut in ¼ lengthwise then in 1-inch pieces	400°F	12-15 mins
Zucchini	2 lbs	Cut in ¼ lengthwise then in 1-inch pieces	400°F	12-15 mins

GRIDDLE CHART

INGREDIENT	AMOUNT	PREPARATION	TEMP	TIME
Griddled cheese sandwich	1 sandwich	As desired	375°F	5-7 mins
Pancakes	4 pancakes (4 inches wide)	As desired	375°F	4-6 mins
French toast	4 slices	As desired	375°F	5-7 mins
Over-easy eggs	6 eggs	As desired	375°F	2-6 mins
Quesadillas	1 quesadilla	As desired	375°F	5-7 mins
Pre-cut fajita vegetables	12 ounces	Pre-cut, thin strips	375°F	10-15 mins
Crab cakes (refrigerated)	4 cakes (10 oz total)	N/A	425°F	8-10 mins
Crab cakes (frozen)	2 cakes (6 oz total)	N/A	425°F	15-18 mins
Hash browns (frozen)	About 4 cups	N/A	425°F	10-15 mins
Pot stickers (frozen)	1 bag (5 oz)	Place flat on tray with ½ cup water	425°F	8-12 mins
Hot dogs	8 hot dogs	N/A	425°F	5-8 mins

DEHYDRATE CHART

INGREDIENTS	PREPARATION	TEMP	TIME
FRUITS & VEGETABLES			
Apples	Cut in ⅛-inch slices, remove core, rinse in lemon water, pat dry	135°F	7-8 hrs
Asparagus	Cut in 1-inch pieces, blanch	135°F	6-8 hrs
Bananas	Peel, cut in ⅜-inch slices	135°F	8-10 hrs
Beets	Peel, cut in ⅛-inch slices	135°F	7-8 hrs
Eggplant	Peel, cut in ¼-inch slices, blanch	135°F	6-8 hrs
Fresh herbs	Rinse, pat dry, remove stems	135°F	4-6 hrs
Ginger root	Cut in ⅜-inch slices	135°F	6 hrs
Mangoes	Peel, cut in ⅜-inch slices, remove pit	135°F	6-8 hrs
Mushrooms	Cleaned with soft brush (do not wash)	135°F	6-8 hrs
Pineapple	Peel, cut in ⅜-½-inch slices, remove core	135°F	6-8 hrs
Strawberries	Cut in half or in ½-inch slices	135°F	6-8 hrs
Tomatoes	Cut in ⅜-inch slices or grate; steam if planning to rehydrate	135°F	6-8 hrs
MEAT, POULTRY, FISH			
Beef jerky	Cut in ¼-inch slices, remove all fat, marinate 8-24 hrs	150°F	5-7 hrs
Chicken jerky	Cut in ¼-inch slices, marinate overnight	150°F	5-7 hrs
Salmon jerky	Cut in ¼-inch slices, marinate overnight	150°F	5-7 hrs
Turkey jerky	Cut in ¼-inch slices, marinate overnight	150°F	5-8 hrs

APPENDIX 2: BASIC KITCHEN CONVERSIONS & EQUIVALENTS

DRY MEASUREMENTS CONVERSION CHART

3 teaspoons = 1 tablespoon = 1/16 cup

6 teaspoons = 2 tablespoons = 1/8 cup

12 teaspoons = 4 tablespoons = ¼ cup

24 teaspoons = 8 tablespoons = ½ cup

36 teaspoons = 12 tablespoons = ¾ cup

48 teaspoons = 16 tablespoons = 1 cup

METRIC TO US COOKING CONVERSIONS

OVEN TEMPERATURES

120 °C = 250 °F

160 °C = 320 °F

180 °C = 350 °F

205 °C = 400 °F

220 °C = 425 °F

LIQUID MEASUREMENTS

CONVERSION CHART

8 fluid ounces = 1 cup = ½ pint = ¼ quart

16 fluid ounces = 2 cups = 1 pint = ½ quart

32 fluid ounces = 4 cups = 2 pints = 1 quart = ¼ gallon

128 fluid ounces = 16 cups = 8 pints = 4

quarts = 1 gallon

BAKING IN GRAMS

1 cup flour = 140 grams

1 cup sugar = 150 grams

1 cup powdered sugar = 160 grams

1 cup heavy cream = 235 grams

VOLUME

1 milliliter = 1/5 teaspoon

5 ml = 1 teaspoon

15 ml = 1 tablespoon

240 ml = 1 cup or 8 fluid ounces

1 liter = 34 fluid ounces

WEIGHT

1 gram = .035 ounces

100 grams = 3.5 ounces

500 grams = 1.1 pounds

1 kilogram = 35 ounces

US TO METRIC COOKING CONVERSIONS

1/5 tsp = 1 ml

1 tsp = 5 ml

1 tbsp = 15 ml

1 fluid ounces = 30 ml

1 cup = 237 ml

1 pint (2 cups) = 473 ml

1 quart (4 cups) = .95 liter

1 gallon (16 cups) = 3.8 liters

1 oz = 28 grams

1 pound = 454 grams

BUTTER

1 cup butter = 2 sticks = 8 ounces = 230 grams
= 16 tablespoons

WHAT DOES 1 CUP EQUAL

1 cup = 8 fluid ounces

1 cup = 16 tablespoons

1 cup = 48 teaspoons

1 cup = ½ pint

1 cup = ¼ quart

1 cup = 1/16 gallon

1 cup = 240 ml

BAKING PAN CONVERSIONS

9-inch round cake pan = 12 cups

10-inch tube pan =16 cups

10-inch bundt pan = 12 cups

9-inch springform pan = 10 cups

9 x 5 inch loaf pan = 8 cups

9-inch square pan = 8 cups

BAKING PAN CONVERSIONS

1 cup all-purpose flour = 4.5 oz

1 cup rolled oats = 3 oz

1 large egg = 1.7 oz

1 cup butter = 8 oz

1 cup milk = 8 oz

1 cup heavy cream = 8.4 oz

1 cup granulated sugar = 7.1 oz

1 cup packed brown sugar = 7.75 oz

1 cup vegetable oil = 7.7 oz

1 cup unsifted powdered sugar = 4.4 oz

APPENDIX 3: RECIPES INDEX

Made in the USA
Las Vegas, NV
06 January 2024

83973776R00044